Pub

in the
YORKSHIRE DALES

Richard Musgrave

• *25 circular walks including country inns* •

DALESMAN

Dalesman Publishing Company
Stable Courtyard, Broughton Hall,
Skipton, North Yorkshire BD23 3AE

First Edition 1996
Reprinted 1997

© Richard Musgrave

A British Library Cataloguing in Publication record
is available for this book

ISBN 1 85568 103X

Printed by Hubbard Print, Dronfield, near Sheffield

Pub Walks

in the

YORKSHIRE DALES

WALKS

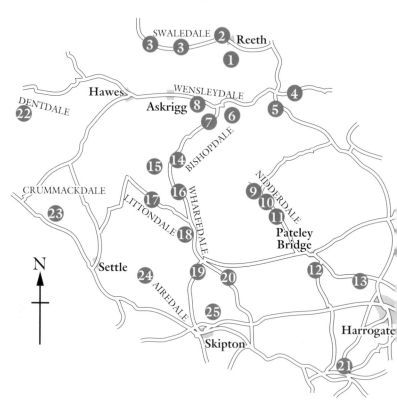

SWALEDALE

Reeth

WENSLEYDALE

Hawes

DENTDALE

Askrigg

BISHOPDALE

NIDDERDALE

CRUMMACKDALE

LITTONDALE

WHARFEDALE

Pateley Bridge

N

Settle

AIREDALE

Skipton

Harrogate

Cover illustration: Tennant Arms, Kilnsey

Cover and pub illustrations
© Geoff Cowton, Glendale Studios, Halifax

Maps by Richard Musgrave and Jeremy Ashcroft

FOREWORD

I've enjoyed being out and about with a decent pair of boots since I was a child. Sometimes it was to exercise the family dog, sometimes for my own exercise, but usually to fuel the almost insatiable curiosity I have for my surroundings.

In the early days this would be in my native Weardale and South Durham then, as my career dictated, in the East Midlands, Essex and for the last nine years in Yorkshire.

During the same period I appreciated the benefits a good pub can offer. The friendly welcome, warmth and shelter and, of course, refreshment. It is not surprising that when planning my walks I've usually fitted in a visit to a suitable hostelry.

When Richard Musgrave asked me to write the foreword on a book of walks in the Yorkshire Dales I had no hesitation, providing he identified at least one pub on each route.

Having walked most of the walks with Richard and, of course, visited all the pubs, I can highly recommend this book and would encourage you to follow Richard's path whenever time permits. As a relaxation from the pressures of modern life I can think of nothing better.

Jeff Lynn
Managing Director
Carlsberg-Tetley North

This book is dedicated to all my rambling friends, with special thanks to Betty Whitaker, Jeff Lynn and Cheryl Pawley for their enormous individual contributions. Thanks also to Ken Smith, Dennis Pearson and Julia and Keith Raw, who assisted with the 'leg work'.

PUBLISHER'S NOTE

BRIDGE INN

*O*nly five miles (8km), yet a delightful ramble, rich in historical interest. The route takes in three upper Swaledale villages: Grinton, Healaugh and Reeth. Contrasting scenery and terrain.

DISTANCE:
5 Miles (8km)
ALLOW:
3 hours
MAP: O.S.
Outdoor Leisure
Map 30
TERRAIN:
Moorland,
meadows and
riverside
PARKING: The
Bridge, by
arrangement.
TEL 01748
884224

The 17th century Bridge Inn, standing by the fast-flowing Swale, formerly served drovers. The inn now prides itself on a warm welcome for everyone and tasty home-cooking, using fresh local produce. Meals are served evening and lunchtime, either in the bar or the quieter dining lounge. Log fires roar and there is plenty to satisfy the real ale enthusiast, as well as those wanting just a tea or coffee.

The area around Grinton and Reeth housed a community of around 7,000 during the boom years of the lead-mining industry in the second half of the 18th century. Numbers fell dramatically when the mines closed almost a century later. The local population is under 1,000 these days.

Leave the Bridge public house, turning right across the road bridge to a tiny gate on the left. Cross the meadows, looking back at the bridge to observe the different shaped arches. This came about when the bridge was widened in the 19th century. The original arch is on the left.

The meadow path leads to Reeth Bridge, from there the road is followed into the village. Leave Reeth to the left of the Buck Hotel, walking along Silver Street. Beyond the business centre and new housing, turn right into a narrow, uneven track – Skelgate Lane. This is followed uphill for almost half a mile (800m), emerging at a gate and giving access onto the moor (G.R. 029 997).

Reeth school has remained operational for more than 200 years. Despite many administrative changes the school is still affectionately known as Reeth Friends' School, indicative of its Quaker origins dating back

to 1780. The school was endowed and built by three brothers - Leonard, George and John Raw, themselves Quakers.

Before striding out across the moor stop and enjoy the wonderful retrospective views of Reeth, Fremington Edge and if visibility permits, Marrick Priory, resting several miles away, east in the valley. The priory, founded in 1154, was a Benedictine (nuns) foundation.

From the gate go straight ahead, towards a pile of stones. Riddings Farm is away to your left. Soon the track meets up with a black gritstone wall and accompanies it for almost three-quarters of a mile (1km). Calver Hill presides to your right.

When the wall abruptly finishes (G.R. 017 996) don't panic - keep straight on, following the wide track. Healaugh, the next port of call, is directly below in the valley. Pass Moorcock cottage then begin the long descent to Healaugh on the access road. Healaugh is a Saxon name Heah - high forest clearing.

Arriving in Healaugh make for the main road but before turning left just beyond West View cottage, make time to visit the village's telephone box, a short distance away to the right.

This red telephone box is quite extraordinary. It contains directories (a rarity in itself) waste paper bin, ash tray and a carpet. There's always a vase of fresh cut flowers too. A wonderful example of local pride. Please leave a small donation.

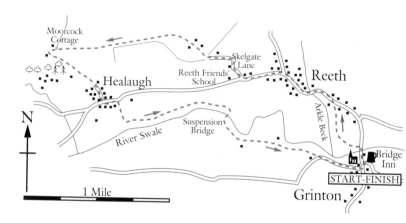

Resuming, follow the main road (left) towards Reeth for a short way. Beyond the last premises on the right swing off the road and enter the fields, passing through a gate (G.R. 019 991). This leads to the bank of the river Swale - turn left for a pleasant mile (1.6km) to Reeth suspension bridge.

The Swale is said to be England's fastest flowing river. As it tumbles eastwards the Swale drops approximately 1,000 feet (305m) during the 27-mile (43.5km) journey from its source to Richmond. Following heavy rain its turbulent waters cause serious flooding in low-lying areas.

Cross over the suspension bridge then turn left, walking

through several fields to arrive at a road for the final 400 metres towards Grinton. The route is obvious and you shouldn't go astray. While in the vicinity of the bridge look across the river - there's much to see. Calver Hill, Reeth School and the long, limestone-clad Fremington Edge are all prominent. Closer scrutiny reveals superb examples of strip lynchets - Anglo-Saxon agricultural field systems dating from the 6-7th centuries. You'll see these 'terraces' in the fields directly in front of Reeth School.

Grinton at first sight seems a little drab and uninteresting but that's not true. There are colourful gardens during summer and an air of friendliness abounds. The village has much to offer historically too. The early Norman church dedicated to St. Andrew was once the only church in upper Swaledale. The parish covers 38,000 acres! St. Andrew's church was referred to as the Cathedral of the Dale. A visit is a must.

BUCK HOTEL

The busy tourist village of Reeth in Swaledale is the starting point for an easy ramble which leads across three superb bridges. Two of these cross the Swale, the other crosses Barney Beck - a spectacular highland watercourse.

DISTANCE:
5½ miles
(8.8km)
ALLOW:
3 hours
MAP : O.S.
Outdoor Leisure
Map 30
TERRAIN:
Easy
PARKING:
Large parking
area in Reeth

The Buck Hotel (01748 884210) is in the beautiful Swaledale village of Reeth. Once a coaching inn and also frequented by northern cattle drovers, the hotel has been in existence since c1750. The premises were formerly known as the Buck Inn.

An a la carte menu of home-cooked, traditional meals is served all year in the restaurant and bar, at lunchtime and in the evening. Traditional hand-pulled real ales are available.

These days Reeth is solely dependent on tourism but 150 years ago everything was quite different. At that time the village was the centre of much lead-mining activity and around 7,000 people lived and worked in the area.

From the cobbled area leave the village via the ginnel beyond Barclays Bank. At the end of the ginnel turn left then right into a lane which passes the doctors' surgery, before veering left, downhill to a gate alongside a barn. Notice the "terraced" areas in the adjoining field.

These are Anglo-Saxon field systems, known as strip lynchets. Crops were grown on these terraces by the early inhabitants of Swaledale during the 6th-7th centuries. The strip lynchets can be seen to greater effect from across the river.

Another prominent landmark in the early part of the walk is Reeth School. The school stands proudly above the terraced fields and the doctors' surgery. It was built originally as a Quaker Foundation in 1780 by the brothers Raw.

From the gate veer right across the fields towards the suspension bridge. Cross the bridge and turn right,

following the river upstream for a long mile, until the path joins a metalled road which is followed to the right unerringly to Scabba Wath Bridge (G.R. 006 983) - a superb triple-arch construction, which carries very little traffic these days.

Cross the bridge, turn left through the stile, eventually following on the main road (take extreme care) for about half a mile (800m) until a gated stile, signposted Healaugh, is encountered on the right, close to a cottage

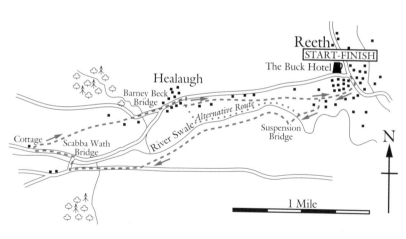

(G.R. 001 985). This is the turning point of the walk.

A degree of common sense is called for throughout the ensuing mile to Barney Beck Bridge. The path is clearly indicated on the map - but not on the ground! The secret is to locate the gap stiles in the walls. From the previously mentioned stile swing right, heading east, across six enclosures, making towards Barney Beck High Bridge (G.R. 014 988) - the third bridge of the outing.

A gated stile leads from the fields, down to the bridge.

Cross the bridge and follow the narrow road into the village of Healaugh, a Saxon name (Heah) meaning a high-level forest clearing. Notice the well-tended telephone box en-route. Careful inspection reveals a carpet, waste paper bin, ash tray, directories and a display of fresh flowers. Wonderful local pride! Do leave a donation.

Continue through the village, heading towards Reeth then leave the road on the right beyond the last building. Here (G.R. 019 991) a choice of routes is presented. It's decision time!

One route meanders through the meadows directly ahead, linked by a series of stiles, following a well-trodden route, and eventually rejoins the lane close to the doctors' surgery. The other option lies down to your right through a gate. Walk along the field close to the wall. This leads to the river - turn left and follow the river back to the suspension bridge before retracing earlier footsteps into Reeth. Each is a pleasant, uncomplicated way to finish off this ramble.

Pleasant ramble visiting two of Swaledale's well known villages - Gunnerside and Muker, also the hamlets of Ivelet and Rash. Refreshments can be obtained at either pub.

DISTANCE:
6½ miles
(10.5km)
ALLOW:
3½-4 hours
MAPS:
Outdoor Leisure
Map 30
TERRAIN:
Easy
PARKING:
Car-parks at
Gunnerside and
Muker

Situated in the former lead-mining village of Gunnerside, The King's Head is thought to have existed since 1697. A full range of bar meals and sandwiches is available lunchtime and evening. Additionally "specials" from the blackboard are offered on a daily basis. Meals are available every day 12-2pm, 7-9pm high season and public holidays; 12-2pm, 7-9pm (except Mondays) low season. Tel 01748 886261.

The last public house in Swaledale westwards, the Farmer's Arms offers snacks and bar meals (12-2.30pm and 7-9pm) all year. It has slightly restricted opening hours during winter. The Farmer's has long been renowned for its beer and lager served in the stone-floored bar. Muker is at the mid-point of the walk. Tel 01748 886297

The village's popularity was rekindled during the 70s and 80s, when it was used as a location for the BBC's All Creatures Great and Small. Gunnerside is also a splendid centre for walking.

From the King's Head cross the bridge and enter the lane
to the left of the post office. Leave Gunnerside via the
primary school and sheltered housing complex, heading
west through a succession of meadows linked by gap-
stiles. The way is straightforward and problems shouldn't
occur. A mile and a half (2.4km) along the valley the
hamlet of Ivelet is entered, shortly after passing through a
superb wooded ravine which is generously sprinkled with
wildflowers in season.

Walk along Ivelet's 'high street'. Note the beautiful carved
door at the last cottage on the left. Turn left at the
junction and follow the road alongside the river Swale to

arrive at the splendid Ivelet Bridge (G.R. 934 977). This is an architectural gem! The bridge isn't the widest arch I've seen in the Yorkshire Dales, but it is definitely the highest. It is a no-go area for long-wheelbase vehicles! The bridge is said to be haunted by a headless dog - so don't worry it can't bite you! Note the flat stone on the ground at the northern end of the bridge. This is where coffins were 'rested' by mourners treading the Corpse Road to Grinton.

In 1580 a church was built at Muker. Prior to this those requiring a Christian burial had to be carried manually to St. Andrew's church, Grinton. Keld is 14 miles (22.5km) away, Muker 10 miles (16km) and Gunnerside 7 miles (11.2km). The route these corteges followed became known as the Corpse Road.

Cross the bridge, following the road uphill to reach Oxnop Bridge. The stream on your right is Oxnop Gill, another location richly spiced by wildflowers in season. Several waterfalls enhance the sylvan beauty.

On reaching Oxnop Bridge turn right then left through the stile at the end of the bridge. The way ahead is easy to follow, steadily rising, on a well-defined path, passing a telegraph pole (100m to the right). The path skirts the pronounced mound heading towards the well-concealed Oxnop Hall Farm (Low Oxnop). Pass through a stile (prior to reaching the farm) then head uphill to another stile in a wall alongside a plantation. Oxnop Hall Farm will be on your right throughout this section.

From this point go diagonally left across a rough pasture to a yellow way-marked gate which gives access onto the

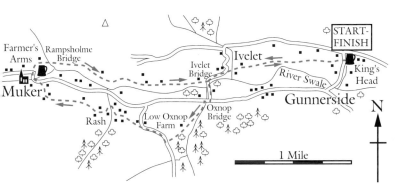

Askrigg Road (G.R. 928 970). Turn right heading downhill to a gap-stile on the left just beyond a road sign.

Careful navigation is required between this point and the tiny hamlet of Rash (G.R. 921 974). Head across the field towards the wall on your right. After about 250m there's a way-marked gate. Pass through this then almost at once swing right through a second gated stile (G.R. 924 973). The view from this point is quite staggering, considering the low altitude.

Go straight ahead, down the field, to a stile at the LEFT of the barn. After this veer right to another stile then, when the path divides, head right to follow the wall downhill by some rowan trees.

Soon after crossing an enclosure is a white cottage - walk down the drive to the gate then turn left into the 'hidden' hamlet of Rash (G.R. 921 974). Continue between the buildings (notice on the left adjacent to the last building on the right the old, stone grinder about 2ft 6in (76cm) in diameter). Beyond the last building pass through the metal gate directly ahead and obey the sign which states, "Keep to the wall on the right".

A clear path soon unfolds and no further instructions are necessary. After 15 minutes you enter an enclosed lane, turn right to Muker (G.R. 910 978), the half way point. Refreshments and toilets are available, and some comfortable wooden benches add to Muker's hospitable charm. Buildings of note are the Literary Institute and St. Mary's church.

Although often reluctant to leave this old fashioned, colourful village, the real attraction of this ramble quickly becomes evident as Muker is left behind.

Take the footpath to the right of the post office and follow it through the meadows to Rampsholme Bridge (G.R. 911 986). From the bridge swing right, eventually walking through a succession of meadows eastwards, all the way to Gunnerside. The footpath is never far away from the River Swale as far as Ivelet Bridge. From that point retrace your earlier footsteps to Gunnerside and refreshments at the King's Head.

OLD HORN

Easy walking, scintillating scenery; the route meanders through meadows and open parkland - features synonymous with lower Wensleydale. The walk concludes with an exquisite section in the company of the rivers Ure and Cover.

DISTANCE:
8½ miles
(13.7km)
ALLOW:
4½ hours
MAP: O.S.
Pathfinder 630.
Middleham and
Jervaulx Abbey
TERRAIN:
Easy
PARKING:
Roadside

The Old Horn is a lovely 17th century building, reputed to have been a farmhouse frequented by local farmers. Local lore reveals a horn was blown to signal meal times, hence the establishment's name. House specialities include steak and kidney pie, giant Yorkshire puddings and the awesome "mighty mixed grill"! Food is served all year, 12-2pm Tuesday to Sunday, and 7-9pm daily. Tel: 01969 622370

With backs to the Old Horn turn right, walking along the road away from the village. After half a mile (800m), at a signpost on the right (G.R. 142 884), swing into the fields and veer diagonally left, crossing two fields before joining the riverside footpath and following it downstream to Ulshaw Bridge (G.R. 145 873).

The bridge stands on the

S P E N N I T H O R N E ,   W E N S L E Y D A L E

site of a Roman ford, part of the Catterick-Bainbridge (Virosidum) road. The remains of a small Roman garrison which guarded the ford can be found to the rear of Ulshaw Grange.

Don't cross the bridge, enter the lane directly opposite as you emerge from the fields.

Immediately on the left, behind the large house, is the tiny Catholic chapel, built by Sir Simon Thomas Scrope (pronounced Scroop) in 1851. The chapel, dedicated to St.

Simon and St. Jude, was endowed and maintained by the family until Mr. R. L. Scrope passed it to the Diocese of Middlesbrough around 1947. The Scrope family burial ground is nearby.

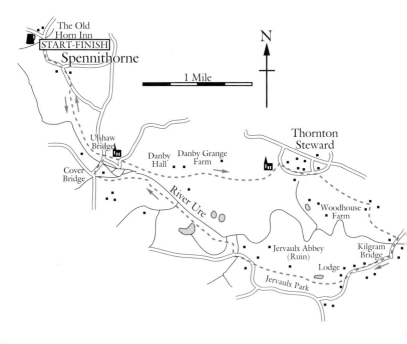

Continue along the road until a pronounced bend then leave the road and follow the river. The track takes you past the confluence of the rivers Ure and Cover, the latter losing its identity, then the ruinous Danby Mill (G.R. 154 870).

Pass through the gate alongside some cottages, then

proceed along a well defined track, swinging away from the river and making towards Danby Hall, the family seat of the Scropes for upwards of four centuries.

Keep following the main track but when it veers left to the house continue straight on to a waymarked stile 500m beyond (G.R. 161 871). Keep walking with the boundary to your right, passing through a succession of waymarked gates. Danby Grange Farm is away to the left and is to be ignored.

After passing through a fifth gate the boundary wall should now be to your left. After passing the next gate the wall ends and is replaced by a wire fence. Soon Thornton Steward church, dedicated to St. Oswald, comes in to view. A visit is highly recommended.

The church is pre Norman and like the village it serves stands on a prominent mound, overlooking a southern aspect of lower Wensleydale. The church and the village are half a mile (880m) apart, similar to the churches at Redmire and Finghall, also in Wensleydale. One explanation of the churches' isolation is that the plague may have wiped out the villages which formerly surrounded them.

Leaving the church either follow the church drive or swing hard left at the gate, to enter a copse and follow a narrow path, heading diagonally right for a short distance to enter a meadow.

Follow the same line across the meadow, making for a signpost at the edge of some trees well below a modern barn. This leads onto the church drive which as mentioned could be followed if preferred - although doing so, you'll forfeit the superb retrospective views which are enjoyed crossing the meadow. The panorama includes the conifer cloaked Witton Fell and the dominant, flat-topped Penhill.

Almost at once the tidy village of Thornton Steward is entered (G.R. 179 871) - what a peaceful place. The eminent Victorian author Edmond Bogg described it as "the most rural of villages" - an accurate, long lasting portrayal. Proceed through the village passing the water pump, then opposite the shelter and phone box veer right at a signpost, leaving the village in a S. direction, making for Woodhouse Farm (G.R. 187 867).

The way across the fields demands careful observation. Seek the white poles which identify the stiles.

As Woodhouse Farm is approached swing 90 degrees right through a gate, proceeding straight on through the field to reach a second gateway where there is a large oak. Follow the boundary hedge (close to the tree) through another gateway, then after 50m turn left, crossing several enclosures to arrive at Kilgram Bridge (G.R. 192 860) - the half way point and a wonderful location for light refreshment.

Resuming, cross over the bridge and follow the road for about half a mile (800m), passing Kilgram Grange and Lane House farms along the way.

Leave the road at a bend where a sturdy lodge house with five chimney stacks stands (G.R.184 855). A signpost confirms the way into Jervaulx Park.

The ensuing mile (1.6km) needs little explanation - simply follow the wide track, eventually passing the scant remains of a once highly impressive Cistercian Abbey, founded in 1156. Notice the arms of the Abbots of Jervaulx, incorporated into a black painted metal gate, close to the SW corner of the ruins.

Beyond the abbey, close to the main gates, is Jervaulx Hall (G.R. 169 858).

Leaving the monastic grounds behind, turn right to follow the road until the boundary wall ends and a road bridge crosses Harker Beck. Swing right, treading a track leading to the riverside - turn left.

Now follows a wondrous two miles (3.3km) in the close company of the rivers Ure and Cover, eventually arriving at Cover Bridge (G.R. 145 870).

Temptation beckons at this location! Try to resist - the Old Horn is only a mile (1.6km) distant.

Cross Cover Bridge, veering right at the road junction. Cross Ulshaw Bridge noticing the large sundial dated 1674, before swinging left and retracing earlier footsteps to Spennithorne.

East Witton, the start and finish point, is a typical Wensleydale village; long and straight, with houses either side of the green. It rests peacefully beneath Witton Fell. Middleham, at half way is the refreshment stop.

DISTANCE:
5 miles (8km)
ALLOW:
3 hours
MAPS: O.S.
Pathfinder Sheet
630 Middleham
and Jervaulx
TERRAIN:
Riverside and
meadows
PARKING:
Roadside,
around green

The Black Swan is a 17th century (grade II listed) traditional inn, offering a character-rich bar, open log fire and a wealth of oak beams. Situated in the historical Wensleydale town of Middleham, the Black Swan offers a wide variety of sandwiches and bar meals. Additionally, a comprehensive a la carte menu is presented in the dining room. House specialities include high quality steaks and the increasingly popular "tipsy casseroles"! There's also a floodlit beer garden for dining 'al fresco' in summer. Tel **01969 622221**

From the bottom end of the village walk to the right of the village green. Instantly, a huge stone bearing a date of 1859 is encountered. This is the Boulder Stone, thought to weigh three tonnes, and marks the site of the village's water supply in times long past.

Continue beside the green until East Witton's tiny Methodist chapel (G.R. 143 860) is reached - swing right, following a signpost to Cover Bridge. The way to the bridge is initially in a direct line, passing through several enclosures with the boundary to your right.

Reaching a ruined barn (signposts) turn right, then left, pass through a gate then cross a field to a second gate. Now head diagonally right towards Cover Bridge which is in sight. Arriving on the road at Cover Bridge (G.R. 145 870) turn left, crossing the bridge to a stile on the left, immediately beyond the public house.

This gives access to a wonderful riverside section which lasts for almost a mile (1.6km) (the key to this ramble is a set of huge stepping stones - be vigilant!)

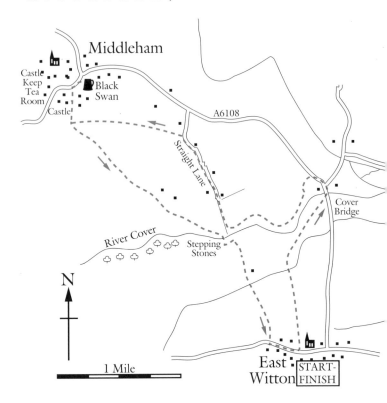

These stepping stones lay just beyond a stile. When you arrive at this point DON'T cross the stile, instead turn 90 degrees right, away from the river, up an incline with the boundary to your left. Check this and get it correct.

Follow this boundary towards a roofless barn, where a gate gives access into Straight Lane. Spennithorne Hall, a salmon-coloured building, and the village church are visible about a mile (1.6km) ahead. Ignore the entrances to private residences which appear first to your left, followed later by a house on the right called Chapel Fields. About 100m short of the lane's end, close to a wooden building on the right, swing 90 degrees left through a waymarked gap-stile (G.R. 133 876) and follow the wall to your right. The path leads uphill towards an angle in the boundary wall - at this point veer left to another waymarked gap-stile alongside a large sycamore. Over the wall is a cricket ground and a superb view of Middleham Castle.

From the stile continue along an obvious path to a second stile. This leads into a hedged avenue, dividing what are thought to have been the castle's gardens. At the end of this delightful section turn right, continuing past the impressive ruin, to enter Middleham via a narrow alley straight ahead. A black metal bollard confirms the way. The Black Swan is on the right.

Take note of your entry into the village - for you'll depart using the same route. The Castle Keep tea rooms are highly recommended for a future occasion!

Middleham is steeped in history and tradition. Richard III resided at the castle for 12 years, during which the village became known as the Windsor of the north. The village also has extensive links with the Turf, housing some dozen or more horse training establishments. Middleham is often compared with Newmarket.

Resume the walk, leaving via the same alley by which you entered. Continue to retrace your earlier footsteps alongside the castle, but instead of turning left into the hedged avenue just beyond "Canaans" bungalow, make to

the gate at the end of the lane (G.R. 127 874). Yorkshire
Water pipeline services have been active in the field to be
crossed. The general line is to head diagonally left across
a huge field, where two gates, almost adjoining, will be
found in the corner. The one on the right has a waymark
to guide you across the next enclosure to a stile alongside
a large tree.

It's the same procedure in the next field - head for the
waymarked gate in the far corner. From the stile follow
the wire fence to your right, cross a track coming in
uphill on the right and head towards a large ash
encompassed in a wall - swing right downhill to the
previously mentioned stepping stones. (G.R. 137 867).

Cross over the stepping stones, pass through a gate and
turn left. After a few metres a waymarker beckons you
away from the river - veer right. Don't use the stile
straight ahead. The signpost confirms East Witton is up
the incline as described.

At the top of the short incline pass through the double
stile then continue along the field with the boundary
close to your right. An old corrugated iron barn stands
resolutely across the field and is to be ignored. By
sticking to the boundary, a second stile is in the top right
corner of the field. From here the houses of East Witton
are in view and your expedition is almost at an end. A
further stile and two gates lead you safely onto the road,
where a left turn leads to East Witton.

FOX AND HOUNDS

An easy walk starting from the unspoilt village of West Burton, featuring a superb waterfall, packhorse bridges and splendid views of the secretive Walden Valley.

DISTANCE:
6½ miles
(10.5km)
ALLOW:
3½ - 4½ hours
MAPS: O.S.
Outdoor Leisure
Map 30
TERRAIN:
Easy, lots of
narrow stiles
PARKING:
Around village
green

The Fox and Hounds is the only remaining public house in the picturesque Bishopdale village of West Burton. It sits alongside the village green, offering all the charm and character associated with a 200-year-old inn. The pub developed from being one of five beer houses in the village during the 18th century - a far cry from its present stature. A comprehensive range of sandwiches and bar meals are available lunchtime and evening all year. Tel 01969 663279

The precise location of West Burton is always a highly contentious issue. Perhaps the reason is the village is such an attractive place and everyone locally wants to be associated? Whatever the reason West Burton is a pretty village and its residents are justifiably proud of their neighbourhood.

The village layout is typically Wensleydale. Long and narrow, with its dwellings either side of the green. A chapel not a church, another Wensleydale feature.

Another fervently supported opinion discloses an allegiance to the Walden Valley, the village being referred to as Burton-cum-Walden. Advocates of this ideal eagerly point out that Walden Beck flows through the village hoping to justify their judgement. Each of these theories bears a degree of credence but it's generally accepted that West Burton truly belongs to Bishopdale. The village connected to the outside world by the B6160 road, proudly flaunts a "Sunday" name - Burton in Bishopdale.

From the Fox and Hounds cross the green, bear left then right, beyond a castellated building at the lower end of the village. This leads to the first attraction of the day -

the wonderful Cauldron Falls. Cross the packhorse bridge (G.R. 019 867) turning left and climbing to a small gate. Pass through the gate continuing to a boundary angle - signposted Rookstone Bridge and Cote Bridge, the next objective.

Proceed through several way-marked stiles through pastures, ignoring Rookstone Bridge (footbridge) on the way to emerge at Cote Bridge (G.R. 018 856). At this point turn left and follow the road for about a mile (1.6km). The road is straight and offers pleasing views of the scenic Walden Valley, including the return pathway far below.

At a pronounced bend leave the road in favour of the farm access track to Whiterow Farm (G.R. 016 836). Pass in front of

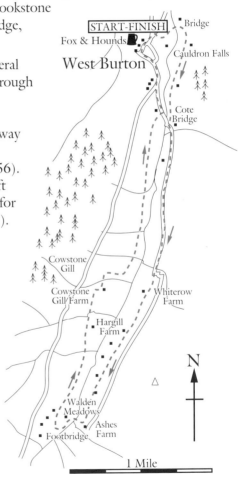

37

the farmhouse, then veer off to the right and pass
through a gate. Go left of a large barn and continue
along the valley, through a succession of gates and stiles
to arrive at Bridge End Farm - renamed Walden
Meadows (G.R.007 824). This is the turning point of
the outing.

Access to the front of the house, after crossing the
footbridge, is gained by veering left up a banking to a
stile set into the wall, left of the house. Head off across
the front of the house towards a white gate (there's a stile
left of the gate). A clear path rises steadily towards
Hargill Farm (G.R. 008 831) then continues to a second
farm, Cowstone Gill House (G.R. 009 835). To reach
Cowstone Gill House leave the main track, passing
through a gate on the right. Veer left of the house to
cross Cowstone Gill at a small bridge. Head straight up
the facing embankment, cross a stile and accompany the
wire fence downhill to a gate - turn left.

The ensuing two miles (3.3km) back to Cote Bridge is
dominated by stiles - dozens of them! Arriving back at
Cote Bridge turn left and follow the road back into West
Burton.

GEORGE INN

Don't be put off by the initial stiff incline, this walk contains some fine views, historical and architectural interest and a short detour will satisfy those wanting to take in the magnificent Aysgarth Falls.

DISTANCE:
4 miles (6.4km)
ALLOW:
2 hours
MAPS:
Outdoor Leisure Map 30.
TERRAIN:
Easy after steep start
PARKING:
Behind village hall

The George was built in 1732 and is Thoralby's only surviving inn. A cosy atmosphere awaits, complemented by good food and open fires. Bar meals and sandwiches are available in the summer between 12-2.30pm and 6.30-9pm; winter 12-2pm and 7-9pm. Closed Tuesday lunchtime. Tel 01969 663256

Thoralby is a large, sprawling village at the northern end of Bishopdale, just a mile (1.6km) short of the ever-popular tourist "Mecca" of Aysgarth.

It's a friendly place, consisting of a mixture of old and recently renovated dwellings. The village has a thriving community and has retained its village hall, post office, and of course the pub.

With your back to the George swing right along the road. Notice the ancient datestones incorporated in the nearby buildings - the village hall (1705), then a dwelling on the right displaying I.B. 1653 are two examples.

Immediately after passing a house on the right which is "decorated" green, turn right into an uneven lane. This lane rises steeply, so no rushing please. There's a signpost Busk Lane 4, Aysgarth 1¼.

The incline is steep, but the retrospective views are tremendous. Penhill and Wassett Fell tower above the Bishopdale villages of Thoralby and Newbiggin. At a pronounced left-hand bend (G.R. 995 868) leave the track, proceeding through a metal gate (concreted drive). From here continue uphill towards a signpost alongside a second gate.

The hard work is now over. Take a rest, then continue across the field, following the exact line indicated by the signpost. Almost at once a yellow waymarker will be seen in the centre of the field, close to a ruined wall. Continue in the same line to a gate in the far corner of the field. From this head downhill to another gate which gives access into Folly Lane - a walled track. Careful navigation of a stream is sometimes necessary!

Head along this lane then, prior to a barn, turn right at a signpost on the right - Aysgarth (G.R. 995 875). Twelve fields lay ahead, each entered and departed by gap stiles.

Stride out across the first field towards a signpost then leave the field through a large gap in the wall. A clear path leads to a stile. From this make diagonally left, eventually locating a stile to the right of the large barn.

From here use a well-trodden path across the fields to a gap in the wall. Another stile leads across the field slightly left to a little gated stile. Continue on to the next stile just left of the telegraph pole. It's easy to follow - pleasant walking too. Yet another gated stile follows and,

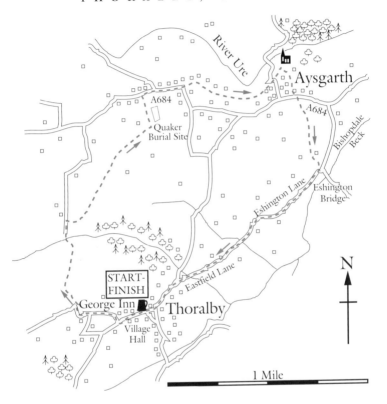

walking close to the wall, Aysgarth village and far off Castle Bolton come into view to the left - Penhill always dominant, accompanies you on the right.

After passing through two well-constructed, but exceedingly narrow stiles, (typical Wensleydale constructions!) there is another gap-stile across the field to the left of a large tree. From here veer left towards a black gate - not the blue one - and follow the track directly to Aysgarth. As you approach the houses notice the enclosed Quaker burial ground (G.R. 003 884) on the right. A plaque on the entrance reads Friends' Burial Ground 1703.

Pass through a final gated-stile then turn right towards the village. It's best to walk on the left where there's a footpath. Take extra care crossing the busy main road.

Opposite the post office notice the Coronation Memorial 1911, the village stocks and also a Silver Jubilee marker, 1952-77. Just a few paces beyond these there's a seat commemorating the Coronation of Elizabeth II in 1953

and the war memorial on the village green. Veer left here, soon passing a cottage named Greystones. Pass Aysgarth Methodist church and continue downhill until the road swings right and ends at a gate. Pass through the gated-stile and at the following stile swing left and follow through a succession of stiles to reach Aysgarth church, St. Andrew's (G.R. 013 885). (Those wishing to see the waterfalls can make a short detour at this point, by turning left at either the road or the church tower.)

A visit inside the church is highly recommended if only to see the rood screen which was carried manually from Jervaulx Abbey at the Dissolution. Boots off please!

The walk continues by following the avenue of limes directly facing the church doorway. At the end of the lane cross the main road to a stile - signpost Eshington Bridge a third of a mile (536m). As you progress across the field, West Burton village appears, nestling beneath Penhill and Wassett Fell. A succession of easy-to-locate stiles lead to Eshington Bridge (G.R. 016 877). Don't cross the bridge, instead swing right into the metalled lane, Eshington Lane/Eastfield Lane. This is followed all the way back to Thoralby. Entering the village notice the fine Georgian household on the right - Wharncliffe - and the former Methodist chapel, dated 1889.

GEORGE AND DRAGON

AYSGARTH, WENSLEYDALE

Splendid walking, with woodland and riverside sections, taking in Aysgarth's lower waterfalls and superb Wensleydale scenery.

DISTANCE:
5 miles (8km)
ALLOW:
2½ hours
MAPS: O.S.
Outdoor Leisure
Map 30.
Stile Maps -
Aysgarth area
TERRAIN:
Easy. Well-
defined tracks
throughout
PARKING:
Lay-by off the
A684, 100m
beyond the
George and
Dragon

The George and Dragon lies just a short walk from the famous Aysgarth waterfalls, on the A684 midway between the market towns Leyburn (Friday) and Hawes (Tuesday). Originally constructed in the 17th century, the building is grade II listed. Internally, much of the original character has been retained. Timber beams, open fire and antique furniture enhance the homely atmosphere. The bar area is decorated with pencil sketches of local "celebrities". A comprehensive range of sandwiches, bar meals, salads and light snacks are available lunchtimes and early evening. Check availability in winter months. Tel: 01969 663358.

Start from the lay-by, following the main A684 road west out of the village (facing the main road, turn left). When the road splits select the left fork - Thornton Rust. Follow this secondary road for about half a mile

(800m), then swing into a wide lane on the left. A large barn confirms the location (G.R. 996 882). This is High Lane.

Soon after a pronounced right-hand bend there is a junction - swing left into an enclosed track known as Folly Lane. Follow this to its conclusion - extra care at the stream! From the gate head uphill, veering slightly left to another gate.

Superb scenery surrounds as Wensleydale is left behind, and you head diagonally right, across a large enclosure towards Bishopdale. A waymarker sited midway confirms the direction to a gate and signpost (G.R. 994 869). From the gate go downhill to a second gate, then continue down the lane to enter

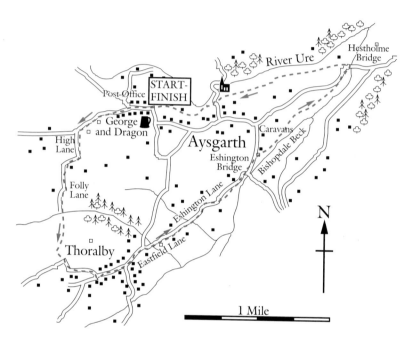

Post Office

START-FINISH

George
and Dragon

High
Lane

Folly
Lane

Thoralby

Aysgarth

Eshington
Bridge

Eshington Lane

Eastfield Lane

Caravans

Bishopdale Beck

River Ure

Hestholme
Bridge

N

1 Mile

Thoralby. Walk straight through the village, passing the public house and post office, to enter a lane which splits off the main road (G.R. 004 870). This is Eastfield Lane, later Eshington Lane. The lane emerges at Eshington Bridge. Don't cross the bridge, take the stile opposite. The way continues for a pleasant mile (1.6km) alongside Bishopdale Beck towards Hestholme Bridge, via a caravan site.

The final 500m towards Hestholme Bridge follows a busy road, so take care. Immediately prior to reaching the bridge cross the road into a farm drive and hop over the stile (G.R. 024 888). Now follows a delightful section alongside the river Ure, taking in Aysgarth's lower falls. Eventually the path leaves the river and enters a small wood before continuing straight through St Andrew's churchyard. A visit to the church is recommended, but clean boots please!

From the churchyard (G.R. 012 885) cross the road to follow a succession of stiles before arriving at a road end/gate. From this point simply follow the road passing Aysgarth Methodist church, to your well earned refreshments at the George and Dragon.

CROWN

Two walks for the price of one here! The A route is a full circuit of Scar House Reservoir; B route terminates short of the reservoir but maintains a great deal of interest.

DISTANCE:
A -8 miles (12.8km). B - 4 miles (6.4km).
ALLOW:
A - 5 hours.
B - 2½ hours.
MAPS: O.S. Outdoor Leisure Map 30
TERRAIN:
Steep ascent on return leg. Not to be walked by unfit persons.
PARKING:
Small car-park beyond pub.

The Crown dates from 1818, incorporating buildings which originate more than a century earlier. The public bar was converted from cottages, the character is still discernable. The darts room was once the home of Ann Rayner, whom some of the locals can remember. The dining room was converted from stables early this century. Between 1960-88 the hotel was used by shooting syndicates as a lodge. In 1988 the hotel and public bar were united to form the Crown Hotel. Sandwiches and bar meals are available lunchtime and evening throughout the high season. Advance enquiries are advised at other times. Tel 01423 755204.

The Crown has become the focal point of village life at the head of the dale. Often you'll encounter local shepherds "talking shop" over a beer and a sandwich.

From the Crown and the adjoining Post Office, swing left to follow the road uphill, out of the village. On the way you'll pass the former school on the right, endowed by Simon Horner in 1803 and built six years later.

Horner died in 1829 aged 93 and is buried in St. Chad's churchyard. Although their family seat was Sunderlandwick Lodge, near Driffield, East Yorkshire, the Horners had long connections with nearby Woodale. The family owned the shooting rights on the surrounding moors.

Soon after passing the tiny car-park the surfaced road
ends and the route continues as a rough, uneven track.
This is In Moor Lane, formerly the road to Coverdale via
the valley now flooded by the waters of Scar House
reservoir. During the drought of 1995 the walls which
enclosed this road were clearly visible.

The route follows In Moor Lane unerringly to Scar
House reservoir. Spectacular aerial views are presented
prior to the descent -
remember though,
you've to come

back the same way! This could be the
terminus for the shorter B route, unless a closer
inspection of Scar House's spectacular masonry is
deemed necessary.

Reaching the bottom of the track (G.R. 065 766) veer

left to pass through the gate. The Tarmaced surface is followed all the way to Angram reservoir, which isn't in sight at this stage. It takes about half an hour's brisk walking before Angram's high profile comes into view. What a splendid sight it is.

Thirteen overflow arches evenly spaced along the embankment of the high, black-stone construction focus the attention at once. Castellated turrets project a fortress appearance. Every detail had been meticulously attended to. Work at Angram commenced late in 1903 and was finally completed in 1918. Behind the embankment, silhouetted against the western skyline is the towering mass of Great Whernside, one of Yorkshire's highest fells. The small, open area to the rear of the modern shelter is where the shops were sited prior to and during the construction works.

Cross the dam then swing right, passing through the broken, iron "kissing-gate", and follow a well-defined track. Within 200m a waymarker confirms the way. Careful inspection reveals the post is made of plastic!

Continue in the same direction until a tumble-down wall is reached - veer to the left side of the wall. A short distance ahead, sited in a depression, is a waymarked stile - cross this, heading in the same direction. *(This area holds water and the going can sometimes be boggy).* Pass through a gap in a wall ahead, continuing with the wall on your right to reach another stile, then 50m ahead there's a ladder-stile (G.R. 047 773). Cross this, swing 90 degrees right to a second ladder-stile, then head downhill, towards the water with the wall on your left.

Towards the bottom of the enclosure swing left at a

gate/stile and proceed along a clear track, passing the shelter. As the path swings right, notice the section of railway line embedded in the ground. Pass through the gate and proceed along the clear track.

Walking with Scar House reservoir to the right, notice the blocks of wood appearing from time to time. These were "sleepers" on the Jubilee line. A narrow gauge railway used to carry materials from Scar House to Angram during the construction period.

This old rail track is followed to the dam at Scar House - ten overflow arches here. Cross the embankment then swing right (if toilets are required veer left) and rejoin the track used earlier. A stiff climb follows as you retrace your earlier footsteps back to Middlesmoor.

CROWN HOTEL

L O F T H O U S E ,　　N I D D E R D A L E

Aqueducts, ancient green lanes, reservoirs in dramatic settings, interesting architecture, waterfalls and spectacular views - this walk has everything.

DISTANCE:
5¹/₂ miles
(8.8km)
ALLOW:
3 hours
MAPS: O.S.
Outdoor Leisure
Map 30
TERRAIN:
Two uphill
sections. Fields
PARKING:
Car-park at
village hall

The warmest of welcomes awaits you at one of Nidderdale's more remote inns. A roaring fire is a hallmark at this fine establishment which is 270 years old. Sandwiches, ploughman's lunches, salads and bar meals are available all year between 12-2pm and 7-9.30pm. Substantial portions are the norm. You've been warned! Tel 01423 755206

From the car-park turn left and follow the road downhill, passing the Crown Hotel to a road junction - turn right. A signpost points the way to Stean and Middlesmoor, both to be encountered later. Cross the road bridge spanning the infant river Nidd, then continue along the road, passing the gateway of Scar House reservoir and the tiny cricket ground where Lofthouse and Middlesmoor entertain during the summer months. Straight ahead at the top of the hill is St. Chad's church at Middlesmoor. Continue along the road until a lane veers off to the left at a bend. It's signposted How Stean Gorge - a well known, much visited, local beauty spot. Keep on this lane, passing some wooden garages, then after crossing a narrow bridge swing left - signposted Ramsgill (G.R.097 734). From the bridge follow the farm access road to Studfold Farm. Immediately beyond the farm buildings swing right, uphill, following an old cobbled lane for almost half a mile (800m). Ignore the left turn, signposted Ramsgill, which soon appears. Where the incline levels out and swings right at a pronounced bend (G.R. 094 728) notice the two aqueducts either side and beyond the ruined barn.

These were erected during the early part of this century, being part of the ambitious Bradford Corporation Waterworks Scheme. This engineering extravaganza conveys water from the two dalehead reservoirs Scar House and Angram, almost 40 miles (64.4km) to Bradford. An ingenious operation.

Stretching out in front at this point is a superb example of a Dales green road - ancient highways, some with monastic connections later used by Scottish drovers moving huge herds of cattle to more lucrative markets in Yorkshire. Approaching one of the aqueducts ignore the obvious left turn, instead swing right 20m farther on to descend to the hamlet of Stean (G.R. 087 735).

Enter Stean after crossing a ford, then proceed along the narrow main road, passing a giant holly tree on the left. Notice a cottage close by, bearing a datestone J I,S 1838. Continue along the road passing the red telephone box, to a stile (Nidderdale Way signpost) to the left of a static caravan. This leads down to re-cross How Stean Gorge at an iron footbridge - a superb location particularly after heavy rainfall.

Climb the "39 steps" then again follow the Nidderdale

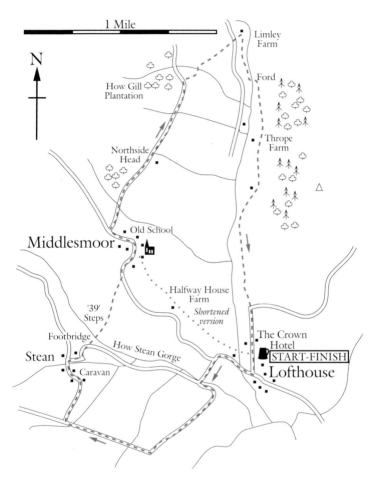

Way signpost diagonally right across the field to another stile. From this stile swing left and follow the wall to your left, passing through several enclosures to arrive at a main road. Middlesmoor church will be prominent as

you cross the fields. At the main road turn left to follow
an uphill course into the village of Middlesmoor
(G.R.093 743). Notice the wonderful views of
Gouthwaite reservoir to the right. After passing the
tastefully-converted Wesleyan chapel, built originally in
1899, an opt out becomes available for those short on
time or eager to return to the pub! (Refer to the final
paragraph of Walk 11, page 61)

The main walk continues through the village (public
toilets) passing the pub and post office. Just beyond these
is an inscription set into the former school wall - it reads:
"This school was endowed in the year MD CCC III
(1803) by Simon Horner Esq., of Sunderlandwick
Lodge and built in MD CCC VII (1807)".

*Sunderlandwick Lodge near Driffield, East
Yorkshire, was the home of the Horner Reynard
family. They owned a 2,640- acre estate in Nidderdale,
comprising Stonesbeck Up and Fountains Earth, until
1862.*

Continue on the road, passing the small car-park,
then 200m beyond the point where the road ceases
to be surfaced swing right along an access road.

*The scenery along this section is superb. Dale Edge
across the valley, Gouthwaite reservoir and
tremendous retrospective views combine to make
this a memorable occasion. Also, look for the
prominent letter "H" emblazoned in the conifer
plantation across the valley.*

Keep on following the access road beyond the
farm, to a point where a new metal gate stands

alongside a copse of pines and rhododendrons. Here pass through the gate and swing immediately right (waymark arrow). Cross the field diagonally left, descending to cross a stream, making towards a stile in the wall, alongside a large tree.

The next stile is cunningly concealed in the wall, 100m to the left of the barn bearing red upstairs doors. From the hidden stile cross the angle of the next field to another stile, then head downhill to another stile, 20m left of the oak tree. The final stile on the section is straight in front and gives access to the Water Authority access road. Turn right.

After 50m swing left into Limley Farm access road. Don't proceed as far as the main buildings, instead swing right at a Nidderdale Way signpost (G.R. 102 758) 50m down the road. Navigate the stile alongside the gate, then veer left to accompany the fence. After crossing another stile follow the riverside footpath, noticing an old lead-mining tunnel to your right after about 25m. After a ladder stile is crossed, proceed in the same direction to arrive at a gate. Passing through this gate cross the river as best you can - there's no bridge.

If the river is in spate simply retrace your steps to the entrance to Limley Farm and follow the Water Authority access road downhill to Lofthouse.

A short distance beyond the river crossing, the path veers away from the river following a depression with a wall to your right. Pass through the double set of gates at the rear of Thrope Farm (G.R.103 752). Usually you'll be greeted from the upstairs barn by a group of barking sheepdogs. Don't be deterred. Thrope Farm is obviously an ancient building, possibly 17th century. The original building on the site was a grange of Fountains Abbey. Limley Farm, encountered earlier, was a grange of Bylands Abbey. The river Nidd was obviously the boundary dividing these vast monastic estates. The last mile (1.6km) to Lofthouse needs little explanation - simply follow the well defined green track to emerge onto a road. At the road turn right, downhill into Lofthouse, and your reward at the Crown Hotel.

YORKE ARMS

RAMSGILL, NIDDERDALE

Highly recommended ramble, visiting five 'up dale' villages. Starting from Ramsgill, the walk is described in a clockwise direction, passing through Stean, Middlesmoor, Lofthouse and Bouthwaite.

DISTANCE:
6½ miles
(10.5km)
ALLOW:
3½-4 hours
MAPS: O.S.
Outdoor Leisure
Map 30
TERRAIN:
Easy. Two uphill
sections. Some
roadwork
PARKING:
Alongside
church wall

The hotel bears the name of the once wealthy Yorke family. The 18th century building was originally used as a shooting lodge for the Yorkes who had acquired much of their wealth from lead-mining in Merryfield Glen, several miles down the dale. The Yorkes sold their entire estate in 1927. It was around this time that the building first became an hotel. The hotel was extensively refurbished in 1993. The Yorke Arms offers bar meals and sandwiches daily all year between 12-2pm and 7-9pm; dinner is 7-9pm; Sunday lunch is 12-2pm. Tel 01423 755243

Leave the village heading towards the farmhouse beyond the telephone box. Locate the Nidderdale Way signpost and proceed through the farmyard. Be careful, don't slip here! Just beyond the farmyard the path forks - veer right. The well-defined track passes through a succession of enclosed pastures linked by enormous ladder-stiles. West House Farm is passed on the left, then about a mile (1.6km) farther on Blayshaw Gill is crossed by a splendid single-arch bridge. A short distance ahead is a major junction - turn left, uphill. Follow this uneven track past Moor House Farm (on the left) to the next major junction on the right (G.R. 087 730).

Turn right downhill along this 'green lane' eventually passing through a farmyard en-route to the hamlet of Stean, a pretty place tucked away out of sight. Follow the road through the village to reach a splendid caravan enclosure - turn left through a narrow gap-stile, signpost Nidderdale Way (G.R. 088 735) heading downhill to cross How Stean Gorge by a narrow footbridge. Stop on the bridge to survey the dramatic limestone formations caused by centuries of erosion.

Leave the bridge and climb the 39 Steps to a gate then cut diagonally right across the meadow, to another gap-stile - turn left uphill to reach the road leading into

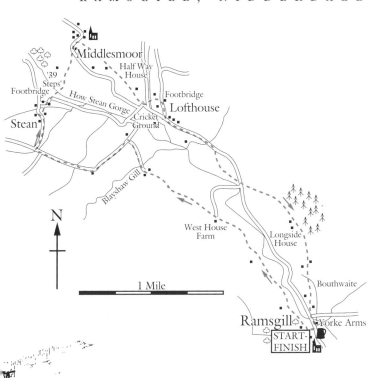

Middlesmoor, the last village in Nidderdale.

Tremendous long distance views of Gouthwaite reservoir and the upper reaches of the dale are available on the way to the church. St. Chad's is said to be the highest church in the Dales. Highest in altitude, not ecclesiastical terms!

Leave the church via a narrow stile and a paved snicket to the right of the gate, then head off down some steps with the next village (Lofthouse) already in sight. Another farmyard (Half Way House) is encountered, keep straight ahead. From the exit gate follow the wall to your right to reach a tiny, well-concealed stile in a corner. After this, several fields are crossed before Lofthouse and Middlesmoor cricket ground is reached. Pass between the ground and a barn on the left. Go straight across the Water Authority road, cross the infant Nidd at a bridge, bearing right towards the village of Lofthouse.

Notice the water fountain, complete with witty inscriptions, proclaiming the virtues of drinking pure water!

Leave the fountain, turning right, and follow the road through the village, past the village hall and pub en-route to a junction - turn left. Follow the road for half a mile (800m) to a signpost/stile on the right (G.R. 106 732). Make diagonally left across a field to a stone ladder-stile then make for the mound of the old Nidderdale railway, which is clearly visible. Turn left along the railway, soon recrossing the road.

Re-entering the field bear right to reach a further stile. Cross this, veer left before a short climb gives altitude and retrospective views of earlier encounters. The way ahead is straightforward passing to the rear of both Longside House (former Youth Hostel), and a farmhouse. Keep the wall on your right for a short distance, to reach a ladder-stile. This leads downhill, into a hidden hamlet of Bouthwaite. Note the splendid 17th century buildings, including Fountains Lodge, which was once a grange (branch office) of Fountains Abbey. Emerging into a lane - turn right. This lane leads directly back into Ramsgill via the bridge.

ROYAL OAK

Old mills are a feature of this pleasant walk which takes in woodland and riverside paths and offers excellent views of an underrated part of Nidderdale.

DISTANCE:
6 miles (9.6km)
ALLOW:
3 hours
MAPS:
Pathfinder - Grassington and Pateley Bridge
TERRAIN:
Easy. Uphill section between Low Laithe and Braisty Woods
PARKING:
Car-park to rear of village hall

The 18th century Royal Oak is a traditional Dales inn. The date inscribed over the door is 1752, although 1730 is displayed on the adjoining stables and coach house, suggesting there was an earlier inn on site. The pub has a cosy bar, open fires, timbered beams etc. A 40-seat restaurant, with wood-burning fire is an additional attraction. Another interesting feature is the numerous quotations, relating to food and drink. The Royal Oak enjoys an enviable reputation for presenting genuine, home-cooked, traditional food. Only fresh vegetables, meat and fish are used. Meals available every day 12.30-2pm and 7-9pm. Not Sunday evening with the exception of June-August. Tel 01423 780200

Leave the Royal Oak - affectionately and accurately described as Nidderdale's Hidden Gem - following the main road to the right, walking in the direction of the church. Soon after passing Wray's coach garage and 200m before reaching the church veer left into Cabin Lane, immediately swinging right - signposted

Glasshouses, a tidy compact village, approximately an hour's walk along the valley. Route finding problems shouldn't ensue as you follow a wide track, passing to the rear of Holy Trinity church. After a short distance the large New York Mill complex appears across the river.

This is the sole survivor of 27 spinning and flax production mills which existed in Nidderdale. At New York acrylic fibres used in carpet manufacture are produced. The mill is owned by Thomas Gill and Sons. Gill senior was an ingenious man. In 1891 he had water-driven turbines installed and New York became the first mill in Nidderdale to have electricity.

After crossing a stream ignore the temptation to swing left when the track forks, keep straight on with the former railway to your right. This path passes alongside a modern bungalow then a small conifer plantation. Across the river the village of Low Laithe can be seen.

After passing through a gate leading out of the wood (this gate is the point to aim for if opting for the shortened version later on), continue to follow the hedge on your right. A second gate is encountered again keep straight on, now following a wall to your right. At this point above the trees on your left is the tall mast on Guise Cliff. Keep following the same line, soon entering the confines of Harewell Hall Farm (G.R. 184 639). Don't proceed towards the main buildings, instead swing off left along the farm access road which is followed all the way to Glasshouses (G.R. 174 645).

The village is easily identified by the tall, needle-like spire of its Methodist church. Glasshouses is reached after crossing the road bridge but almost at once is a signpost

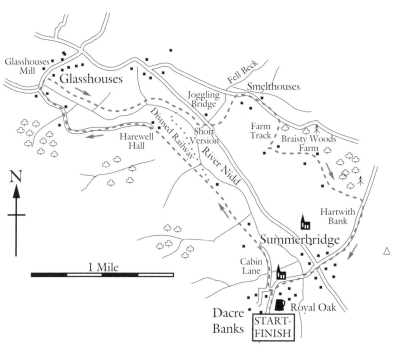

at a gap in the wall on your right, 100m beyond the bridge. This leads through a mill complex.

Notice the differing datestones incorporated into the mill buildings. These no doubt indicate the flax industry expansion period as new, larger premises were required.

When you see a mill building to your left bearing a date of 1852 swing right (signpost Low Laithe) to accompany the mill's external wall, quickly emerging alongside the River Nidd. The next mile and a half (2.4km) treads a wonderful riverside footpath to Low

Laithe (G.R. 193 637) passing a disused viaduct and a footbridge en-route. The footbridge is known locally as 'the joggling bridge' (G.R. 186 642), because it joggles or vibrates as you walk over it. This bridge offers a short cut for those wanting an early finish. (To achieve this cross the bridge, head straight across the field to the old railway track. This can be followed for a short distance, prior to re-entering the wooded area by the previously mentioned gate. From that point simply retrace earlier footsteps to Dacre Banks.)

Continuing beyond the bridge follow the river to its confluence with Fell Beck, here swing left, away from the river, to follow Fell Beck a short distance to a little

footbridge. From the bridge go left across a field to reach the main road which is crossed directly. Take the track to the right of Carter's Knox Manor restaurant to accompany the gurgling waters of Fell Beck all the way to the 'opulent' village of Smelthouses (G.R. 193 644).

Emerging onto the road turn right and follow its course, uphill, for almost half a mile (800m) to a farm access road. As the incline levels out, the jagged skyline to your left reveals the famous Brimham Rocks. Walk along the access road to Braisty Woods Farm (G.R. 196 637) passing between the farm buildings. Beyond these ignore the turning on the right, and head for a junction of tracks just ahead. At this point veer right, there's a signpost for Woolwich on the barn.

The well-defined track is followed to Woolwich Farm (ignore a left fork en-route) with its picturesque duck pond. Pass through the gate beside a large stone barn.

Quite soon (150m) leave the track, passing through a gate close by an implement shed (G.R. 204 633). This leads into the lower regions of Braisty Woods. Dacre Banks is in view away to the right.

Negotiate a finely constructed stone step-stile, then 20m beyond look out for the yellow waymark arrows on the trees. The woodland path isn't difficult to follow and emerges beyond a new building at a road - Hartwith Bank (G.R. 205 626). Turn right and follow the road downhill into Summerbridge. The Royal Oak at Dacre Banks is just a half a mile (800m) away, downhill from the crossroads.

BAY HORSE

This walk contains a wonderful riverside section with typical fine views of Nidderdale and a glimpse of the dale's former connection with mills and railways.

DISTANCE:
6 miles (9.6km)
ALLOW:
3 hours
MAPS: O.S.
Pathfinder 653
and 663
TERRAIN:
Easy. Fine
riverside stretch.
Some roadwork
PARKING: Bay
Horse by
arrangement

Originally an 18th century turnpike inn resting alongside the Wetherby-Grassington road, the family-run Bay Horse has long held a reputation for excellent food and beer. High-quality restaurant, bar meals and sandwiches are available all year. Tel 01423 770230.

The village name is derived from Burnt Gates. The reference being loosely attached to a dispute which arose between monks of Fountains Abbey and foresters working for the estate of Knaresborough Forest. It's thought that during the dispute the toll gates were torn down, damaged or burnt.

Start from the Bay Horse car-park (G.R. 253 613), turning right and follow the road for a short distance to a stile in the wall on your right (opposite a bench). From the stile head diagonally left across the field to a gate giving access to a road (Clint Bank). Follow the road to the right for almost a mile (1.6km). Do take care along this section as the road is often busy.

As you head along Clint Bank be aware of the wonderful views on your right.

At the first major junction turn left into Clint Bank Lane which is followed unerringly to the next village - Hampsthwaite.

On the way you'll pass the village stocks and Clint Cross, renovated in 1977 by Nidderdale Round Table to commemorate the golden jubilee of the Round Table movement, founded by Louis Marchesi of Norwich in 1927.

A short distance beyond the stocks and cross the road forks - bear right to Hampsthwaite. All around, splendid rural scenery typical of lower Nidderdale unfurls. Pass the entrance to Stoney Banks, continuing along the road with the church of St. Thomas Beckett,

B U R N T   Y A T E S ,   N I D D E R D A L E

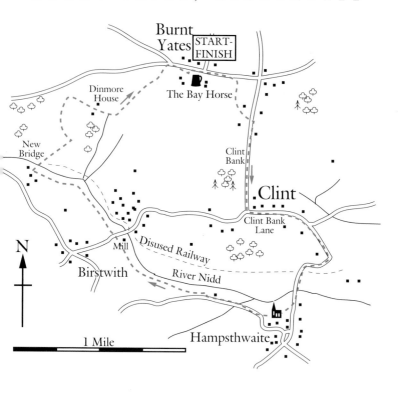

Hampsthwaite, prominent straight ahead. At a sharp
bend on the road notice the remains of a Nidderdale
railway bridge, then continue towards Hampsthwaite via
the road bridge spanning the river Nidd.

*Immediately before the bridge is an inscription set into the
wall on the left by a small seat. It reads Commemoration of
the Jubilee of Her Majesty Queen Victoria, June 20 1887.
This wall was built when the road was widened.*

Cross over the bridge to enter the churchyard, noticing

the 'mice' carved onto the lychgate. Tiny mice were the trademark of Robert Thompson of Kilburn, North Yorkshire - a master wood carver. Presumably he made this lychgate.

The churchyard contains several interesting features including the grave of a well known Leeds brewer - Joshua Tetley.

Pass through the churchyard then follow the adjoining pathway to a road. Turn right along the road for a quarter of a mile (400m), seeking a barn on the right with a Nidderdale Way signpost pointing the way to the riverside. The delightful riverside footpath leads to Birstwith via the legally diverted footpath around the right hand perimeter of the mill complex. It's easy to follow from the new gate on your right just before the mill buildings. Emerging from the confines of Birstwith Mill cross the road, the way ahead again confirmed by a Nidderdale Way signpost.

Once again the footpath accompanies the river and this becomes an exquisite half mile (800m) to New Bridge (G.R. 236 604) - a packhorse bridge built in 1822. This superb construction spans the Nidd, the single arch measuring some 70 feet (21.3m)! Over the bridge continue along an obvious, rising track, which is often very muddy.

This track soon re-crosses the Nidderdale railway. Don't follow the railway, maintain an uphill course, following the telegraph poles to arrive at a gate (G.R. 238 605). Ignore the signpost, instead head off to the left, uphill to a second gate by a large holly bush. It can be difficult to open but there's a knack - pull the gate towards you and lift the catch. Keep on following the narrow lane, (ignore the ladder-stile on the left) until the incline levels out. Fifty metres beyond this point there's a little step stile on the right. Cross the stile into a field, accompanying the wall as far as a telegraph pole. From the pole veer left across the field to a gate leading into the access road to Dinmore House (G.R. 242 607). Turn right.

Follow the road through the buildings - it seems imposing but a right of way exists. Don't be deterred - press onwards. Go between the first two buildings to a gate on the left of Stable Cottage. Continue to a second gate, then a third gate with a stile and a marker post. DO NOT proceed to the fourth gate, instead swing left up a short rise to a gate on the right of a large barn.

On reaching this gate Burnt Yates is in view across the fields. Simply accompany the wall on the left, passing through several enclosures to emerge on the main road. Turn right for a short way to the Bay Horse.

WHITE LION

C R A Y , W H A R F E D A L E

The eminent author Alfred Wainwright described Cray as a "tiny oasis". A fitting description indeed.

A warm welcome awaits at the White Lion (01756 760262) where wholesome, home-cooked food (served in a non-smoking dining room) and traditional hand-pulled real ales are available throughout the year. The White Lion is not at the start of this walk but at a convenient three-quarter point. The inn, on the B6160 road between Buckden and West Burton, was a drovers' hostelry during the last century. Buckden Pike, one of the Dales' highest peaks, watches over the hamlet of Cray.

A highly-scenic ramble centred around the head of one of Yorkshire's most popular dales - Wharfedale. This outing visits three up-dale villages: Buckden, Hubberholme and Cray. It's a popular circuit, well waymarked and navigational problems shouldn't arise.

Leave the car-park, heading towards the village but not into it. Instead cross the road and the village green, making for the stone bridge which

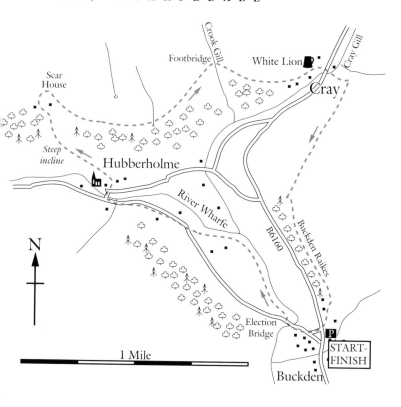

strides the infant River Wharfe. The bridge, known
locally as 'Election Bridge', was built as a bribe for votes
in a local election of 1750.

After crossing the bridge walk along the road for a
short distance, to reach a gate on the right. Follow the
Dales Way sign which points diagonally across the
meadow and leads to a well-defined riverside
path. Watch carefully, wagtail, dipper and kingfisher

are known to frequent this stretch of the river. The riverside path eventually leads back to the road. Turn right and follow the road for a quarter of a mile (400m) to Hubberholme, a small hamlet full of interesting features. The first is the George Inn which was formerly a vicarage. Cross the superb single arch stone bridge, then pass through the signposted gate to the right of the Norman church of St. Michael and All Angels.

A visit inside the church is strongly recommended. If you decide to step inside look out for the mice! Not real ones, but wooden carvings made by the master craftsman Robert Thompson of Kilburn, North Yorkshire. Mice were his trademark and he became known as the 'mouseman'.

Follow the track around the church to an obvious junction - take the right fork. A steep climb ensues,

following a rough vehicle track to Scar House Farm.

A building which formerly stood on this site was a Quaker Meeting House. At the house in 1652 James and Ann Tennant were 'convinced' by George Fox. The datestone from the original building has been incorporated in the present building - J.A.T. 1698. Also, there is a tiny Quaker burial ground nearby.

Leave the farm making for the limestone ridge behind the house and turn right. A delightful half-hour stroll follows, high above the head of Wharfedale. Tremendous views unfurl as a level, well-trodden, grassed path is followed via Crook Gill (waterfalls) to Cray, emerging at the rear of the White Lion Inn - an ideal refreshment stop.

Cross the road opposite the inn, then navigate the beck aided by recently-installed stepping stones - be careful! Pass through a gate then head uphill by the wall to reach another gate - turn right. Initially the way ahead is level, offering wonderful views once again. Soon the path becomes uneven as it descends to Buckden. This concluding part of the walk is known as Buckden Raikes and is part of the Roman road linking the garrison towns of Bainbridge (Virosidum) and Ilkley (Olicana).

GEORGE INN

The tiny church at Hubberholme is worth a visit on its own, but drag yourself away for some of the best views in Wharfedale and splendid waterfalls en route.

DISTANCE:
3 Miles (4.8km)
ALLOW:
2 hours
MAPS: O.S.
Outdoor Leisure
Map 30
TERRAIN:
Easy. Short
uphill section
out of
Hubberholme
PARKING:
Alongside river,
near the church

The George can truthfully be described as a traditional Dales inn. It's a place that reeks of character; white-washed walls, stone-flagged floors, beamed ceilings, open fire - 18th century charm indeed. The inn was used as a cattle shed and a vicarage in years gone by. Solid tree trunks shoved in by a farmer's tractor, support the roof in the top bar, and a massive brown trout caught locally in 1934, adorns the wall. Food is available lunchtimes and evenings throughout the high season. Between November and March, it's advisable to ascertain before setting off. Tel 01756 760223.

Before leaving the George Inn (G.R. 926 783), notice the Victorian post box set into the wall of the pub. It's amazing that the postal service extended into such remote parts of the Dales in those early days of the service.

Cross the bridge spanning the infant river Wharfe, then before going through the gate (signposted Scar House $\frac{1}{2}$ mile, Yockenthwaite $1\frac{1}{2}$

miles) walk on for 10 metres to see an old cast-iron West Riding boundary sign near the base of the wall.

Continue around the church - St. Michael and All Angels, which contains a memorial to the Yorkshire author and playwright J.B. Priestley, and also exhibits work by the master woodcarver Robert (Mouseman) Thompson. Seek out his trademark - tiny mice. One was carved in every piece of his work. The church is also one of two remaining in Yorkshire to have retained a rood loft. The other is at Flamborough. These churches apparently defied an edict issued by Elizabeth I.

Having passed around the rear of the church, almost immediately the path divides. Go right on the route which leads steeply uphill to Scar House Farm which has Quaker connections.

George Fox, the founder of that movement, visited Scar House twice, in 1652 when James Tennant and his family were convinced, and again in 1677. James Tennant died for his faith in York Castle between these visits. The present building was erected in 1876, the datestone bears the initials J.W.R. The datestone from the original farmhouse has been incorporated into the wall above the front porch: J.A.T. 1698 - James and Ann Tennant. The tiny Quaker burial ground lies 20m to the left of the farmhouse, the spot marked by an inscribed stone set into the wall alongside a wooden gate - Friends' Burial Ground, 1650.

Continuing the walk, pass to the left of the house, then swing right to the rear of it. There's a yellow waymark on the barn. Notice the tiny windows in the rear wall! Emerging from the rear of the farm, double back to the

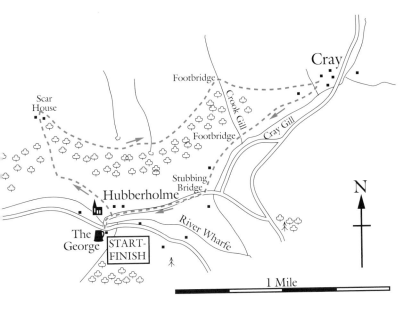

right at a three way signpost, carefully navigating the limestone steps leading to a delightful, high-level grassed pathway that's followed all the way to Cray (G.R. 943 793).

En-route the Wharfedale cairn is encountered away to your left, soon after passing through a broken-down wall where a stile was once sited.

The views at this point are simply magnificent, looking south along Wharfedale and east to the towering mass of Buckden Pike. To your right are numerous limestone pavements. Three colours dominate the landscape on a fine day - green, grey and blue. The greenness of the pastures and hillsides, the varying shades of grey limestone and the clear blue sky above.

A wooden footbridge crosses Crook Gill (G.R. 934 792), after crossing this veer right, still following a well-trodden path that arrives at a gate close to a large barn. Strangely, there's a television aerial at the gate!

Keep straight on, passing to the left of a wall which ends abruptly in the middle of the field, then pass through two gateways beyond it. The first building of Cray appears ahead and when this is reached swing sharp right at the far end of the building into Cray Gill. A signpost indicates the way. Pass through a wooden gate to the left

of the house and head off on a well-walked path, keeping
to the right of a telegraph pole. Twenty metres beyond
the pole the path departs from the limestone ridge on the
right and begins to descend towards another marker post.

Soon the path is alongside Cray Gill's tumbling
waterfalls. This is a superb location. A tiny arched bridge
carries you over Crook Gill again, close to its confluence
with Cray Gill. Simply follow the tumbling water to
emerge at Stubbing Bridge (G.R. 934 784) turning right
to follow the narrow road back to Hubberholme. The
walk is short but highly rewarding.

FOX AND HOUNDS

S T A R B O T T O N ,   W H A R F E D A L E

Starting from the unspoilt village of Starbotton this walk provides some excellent views of Wharfedale for those willing to put in the effort!

DISTANCE:
A Route 5 miles (8km).
B Route 4 miles (6.4km)
ALLOW:
A 3 hours.
B 2¼ hours
MAPS: O.S. Outdoor Leisure Map 30
TERRAIN:
Steep incline on A route
PARKING:
Roadside, where it's safe to do so, and behind the pub near the bridge

A comprehensive menu is available all year at the Fox and Hounds - with certain exceptions. Do check prior to embarking on your ramble, particularly in winter. Food is available 12-2pm. 7-9pm except Monday. The premises are closed all day Monday from November to March and shut down completely for four weeks in January/February. Tel 01756 760269

Starbotton has to be my favourite village in upper Wharfedale. Small and compact, it contains a host of tidy cottages, many of which display colourful gardens during summer. An air of pride exists. Additionally, there's a definite lack of commercialisation - unusual in this part of the world.

Amenities are scarce. Gone are the post office, school and chapel - no public toilets, either. But the village's public house has survived, and despite a succession of owners in recent years, the place seems to be flourishing.

The village is midway between the tourist hot-spots of Kettlewell and Buckden. It rests at the lower end of Cam Gill, a mountain stream which in 1686 wrought havoc on the tiny village after a storm. Many inhabitants of Starbotton and Kettlewell were drowned.

A leisurely stroll around the village gives some indication as to when the rebuilding took place. Many datestone lintels are incorporated into the buildings.

Leaving the Fox and Hounds (G.R. 954 748) veer left along the road, taking note of the datestone opposite T.S. 1665. Pass the telephone box - (thankfully still an old fashioned red one) and the former post office - Post House, on the right. The former chapel is on the left.

Continue along the road for a short way, to a signpost on the right - Arncliffe 2¼, Kettlewell 2, Buckden 2¼. An intriguing selection indeed. Pass through the gate, walk down the lane and cross the footbridge (G.R. 952 745) where a choice of routes is presented. Those electing to undertake the B route, turn left, following the signpost to Kettlewell. This route is well-walked and requires little description. Simply follow the way-marked path. The route doesn't slavishly follow the river. I've never heard of anyone going astray along this section.

The A route offers a challenging steep section and shouldn't be attempted by the unfit or ill-equipped.

If this is your choice, go straight ahead from the bridge - signposted Arncliffe. Almost at once a barn is encountered - swing left. This is the beginning of the stiff, uphill section. It took me half an hour to reach the summit. Take your time. The path is narrow, uneven and initially enclosed between two walls. It also travels through a wooded section and flies can be a problem in season. When you reach a gate the climbing is almost over. The view will adequately compensate your physical efforts. Have a breather, then continue to a second gate (G.R. 952 736).

Stop here to survey the panorama. All the upper Wharfedale villages are spread out below. Buckden away to the left, Starbotton with Cam Gill dramatically illustrated; and away down the valley, right, Kettlewell. A super spot to be!

Pass through the gate, turning left now following the Kettlewell sign - ignore Arncliffe. After crossing a broken wall a farmhouse will be seen ahead. The route through the derelict farm was recently altered and the required waymarking not completed at the time of writing. After passing through a gate just prior to the farm, make for the narrow gate to the left of the buildings. Pass through, veering right to another gate which leads to the front of Moor End Farm (G.R. 954 731) - swing left to the gate between the wall and a barn, then head off on a superb grass track.

Kettlewell is in sight far below and the remainder of the route to that point requires no explanation.

Before you descend note the superb examples of

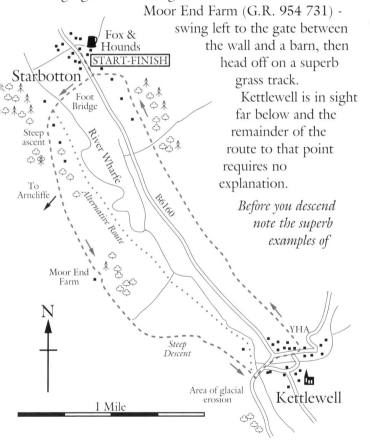

glacial erosion in the form of huge steps on the landscape directly ahead.

Enter Kettlewell, crossing the road bridge, then after spending whatever time you feel necessary, depart via the lane to the left side of the Bluebell Inn (G.R. 968 723). *Both A and B routes tread the same course back.

Following this lane notice the cottage names - Amerdale, Gower, Wharfe and Skirfare (Littondale's river). Leave the metalled surface, where the road bends right, continuing in the same direction to enter an unmade lane between Cam Cottage and Cam Lodge.

Hop over the gated stile then swing left following the wall. As this ensuing section unfurls, look across the valley and enjoy retrospective views of earlier events. Moor End Farm is clearly visible.

The way back to Starbotton needs little description. A succession of eight stiles determines the route.

QUEEN'S ARMS

LITTON, LITTONDALE

Littondale is a quiet, colourful and scenically attractive dale adjacent to Wharfedale. The ramble visits two of Littondale's five hamlets - Halton Gill and Litton.

DISTANCE:
8½ miles
(13.7km)
ALLOW: 4½
hours
MAPS: O.S.
Outdoor Leisure
Map 30
TERRAIN:
One uphill
section -
generally easy
PARKING:
Roadside

Set in the reclusive valley of Littondale, the Queens Arms Inn originates from the 17th century. Known locally as the Queens, it lies within the parish of Litton. The village gives its name to the valley - Littondale - the "lost" dale in the Charles Kingsley's Water Babies. A cheerful welcome awaits, complemented with open fire, oak beams and wholesome country fare. Real ale is served too. Delicious food and sandwiches are available all year. An advance telephone call is recommended out of season. Tel 01756 770208

Just beyond Kilnsey in upper Wharfedale, a road branches off to the left signposted Arncliffe. This is the road into Littondale. Littondale contains five tiny villages sprinkled evenly along the eight miles (12.9km) of the valley.

Travelling north westwards along the dale, Hawkswick is the first village observed. It rests on the east bank of Littondale's river Skirfare, emitting a vision of pride and opulence. This is quickly followed by Littondale's "capital" Arncliffe. Next comes Litton, then Halton Gill and finally Foxup.

With backs to the Queens swing right, heading out of the village. Shortly after passing the tiny post office veer left, prior to the last buildings. A signpost indicates the way down to the river which is crossed by a substantial wooden footbridge. After crossing head diagonally right to a stile set in the wall. This leads across two enclosures to a barn. Pass through the metal gate, turning right to follow an old lane, to arrive at New Bridge (G.R. 898 743) which was built around 1840. Don't cross the bridge, instead pass through the gate.

A brief spell of hard work begins at this point. Treading a section of a former drovers' track to Settle. Initially the incline is steep, though the track soon levels out and offers breathtaking views of Littondale and Hesleden Gill. The view adequately compensates for the physical efforts. Continue along the defined track for about two miles (3.2km) to a metalled road (G.R. 855 728), passing through several gates en-route. At the road turn right.

Walk along the road for a short way until the road passes between a wall - here turn immediately right locating a wooden stile set in a wall 20m ahead. Close by is a site known as the Giants' Graves, thought to be Bronze Age burial sites and re-used in Iron Age times.

Cross the stile then pass through an area of 'clints and grykes' - limestone outcrops - veering half left to pick up a clear path to the left of Hesleden Gill, sometimes known as Penyghent Gill. This is a highly scenic area offering wonderful sights, including a succession of tumbling waterfalls. These will be seen far below the path to the right. This ensuing section is well signposted and

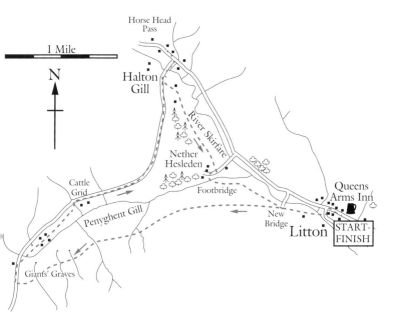

navigational problems shouldn't arise. Eventually the path rises to rejoin the road left earlier.

For the next 1½ miles (2.4km) follow the road towards Halton Gill, (G.R. 880 765) a grey-stone village nestling at the foot of Halton Gill Beck. Our route doesn't take in the village, but a short detour can be made if you wish.

Most of the houses in the village date from the 17th century. The building which was formerly the school and church combined, has a datestone WF 1626. The initials relate to William Fawcett, a dalesman and wealthy wool merchant from Norwich who financed the building. The section used for education was originally the vicarage.

As Halton Gill is approached, try to pinpoint the track creeping up the hillside to the rear of the village. This is Horse Head Pass, an ancient route linking Littondale and the higher reaches of Wharfedale.

Throughout the 19th century Halton Gill's parson conducted services at Hubberholme in Wharfedale. Rev Thomas Lindley fulfilled this role for 40 years between 1807-47. Until his death in his 80th year, Lindley either walked or rode over the Horse Head Pass.

Arriving at the bridge turn right (waymarked Litton 2¼ miles), passing through a succession of meadows to reach Nether Hesleden Farm (G.R. 887 747). From the farm the way back to Litton is straightforward. Again the route is well waymarked. New Bridge, encountered on the outward leg, is revisited as is the old lane to the barns known as Spittle Croft (G.R. 902 741).

One of these dates back to monastic times and is said to have been an outlying hospital on the vast Fountains Abbey estate. The building is identified by the stone-mullion windows.

TENNANT ARMS

KILNSEY, WHARFEDALE

*K**ilnsey Crag dominates the scene in this part of Wharfedale. But the views contain much more with ancient routes, dry riverbeds and evidence of Anglo-Saxon farming.*

DISTANCE:
6¾ miles
(10.9km)
ALLOW:
3-4 hours
MAPS:
Outdoor Leisure
Map 10.
Southern Area
TERRAIN:
Short scramble
at Conistone
Dib. Rest easy
PARKING:
Roadside or by
arrangement
with Tennant
Arms

The Tennant Arms rests at a junction of the B6160 and an old monastic route known as Mastiles Lane, overlooked by Kilnsey Crag - a 170ft (52m) limestone outcrop. The pub was originally built in the 17th century as a coaching inn. The bar, with a stone-flagged floor and open fire, has an extensive selection of hand pulled, traditional ales and freshly prepared bar meals. Tel 01756 752301.

A busy, popular village in upper Wharfedale, Kilnsey is known for and presided over by its famous sphinx-like limestone crag, the haunt of the climbing fraternity. A trout farm and Mastiles Lane - an ancient monastic route associated with the monks of Fountains Abbey - are other local attractions.

From the Tennant Arms turn left along the road for about 250m to a signpost alongside Scar Laithe Barn, indicating the way to Conistone Bridge, which is half a mile (800m) away across the fields, diagonally right. Arriving at Conistone Bridge (G.R. 675 978) turn left along the road towards the village, left of the Maypole. After a few metres leave the road in favour of a light-coloured gravel path which leads towards a white cottage. Keep to the right of the cottage to a gate which gives access to a splendid location - Conistone Dib. Now permanently dry, but a tumbling river many years ago.

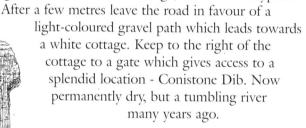

The ensuing mile (1.6km) is rather special, requiring little description. Simply walk one foot in front of the other, crossing a couple of ladder-stiles en-route to the top end of this dry valley. Ignore the signpost to Grassington.

The final 200m rises steeply

and a little handwork is called for, though problems shouldn't arise. At the top of the Dib hop over the ladder-stile and prior to completing a hairpin left turn, stop to admire the view. Kilnsey and its famous crag dominate the lower landscape while Mastiles Lane, snaking over the distant horizon, completes the picturesque

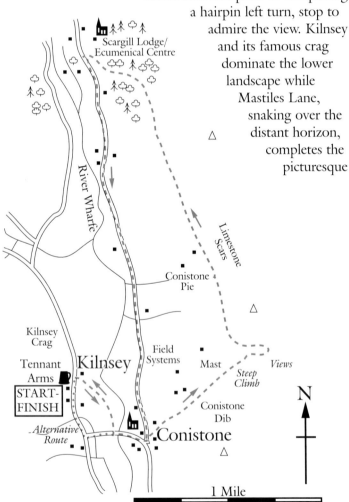

panorama. Resume the walk, passing through the gate and heading off in a straight line to cross the main track. This leads onto a pleasant, level green path - the signpost merely states footpath! Additional clues are the limestone escarpment to your right and an aerial away to the left.

After walking along this superb, high-level track for just 200m, views into Littondale and of Birks Fell and the amusingly named, pork pie-shaped, limestone outcrop Conistone Pie (G.R. 987 687) are presented. On reaching the ladder-stile alongside Conistone Pie, views of upper Wharfedale are presented too. This is a lovely place to be. Continue along this track, negotiating a succession of ladder-stiles. The Tennant Arms lies far below in the valley to your left.

Eventually the path leads you to a conifer plantation, where a gate near the wall will be found. Pass through the gate then head down the track, noticing Scargill Lodge - an Ecumenical Centre - as you descend. This track eventually leads onto a road - turn left. This road is followed all the way to Conistone village. On the way notice the barn bearing a datestone W.C. 1865. Also try to find the superb examples of 'strip lynchets' Anglo-Saxon field systems in the fields. These terraced, crop growing sites are almost opposite to Kilnsey Crag and to your left.

Entering Conistone village a visit to the church of St. Mary is recommended. In the graveyard just beyond the gate is a memorial to six men, aged 17-26, who in 1967 died in a tragic caving accident. Their bodies rest in the sealed-up Mossdale cavern. From the Maypole simply retrace your earlier footsteps back to Kilnsey.

FOUNTAINE INN

LINTON, WHARFEDALE

Packed with interest and variety, the route meanders through the spectacular scenery of the ever-popular Wharfedale. Features include a fairy bridge, waterfalls, a Norman churches and a hidden village.

DISTANCE:
5¹/₂ Miles
(8.6km)
ALLOW:
3¹/₂ hours
MAPS: O.S.
Outdoor Leisure
Map 10
TERRAIN:
Easy
PARKING:
Around village
green

The Fountaine's proprietor proudly boasts no juke box or gambling machines. This is an old-character public house, containing many nooks and crannies. The theme of the pub is ducks! Lots of live ones outside, loads of memorabilia inside.

Only real ales are served, together with excellent pub grub - "Splendid food" (Good Beer Guide 1995). Bar lunches and evening meals are served daily. Tel 01756 752210.

Begin at the Fountaine Inn, named after Richard Fountaine, a local benefactor who built the almshouses at the southern end of the green. Cross the beck by one of the five options available. There's a road bridge, a packhorse bridge, a clapper bridge (footbridge), stepping stones or you can simply wade through the ford - it's not deep normally!

Follow the road out of the village, heading in the

direction of Grassington. Soon after passing the Men's Reading Room on your left, there's a cross-roads - go straight ahead. Continue downhill to a ginnel immediately before the large building - formerly a silk spinning mill converted to residences in the early 80s. The ginnel leads to the impressive Linton Falls which are crossed via the substantial footbridge. Before negotiating the falls notice the "tiny fairy" bridge a few steps into the ginnel.

This bridge is known as Li'le Emily's Bridge, named after Emily Norton, a local girl featured in Wordsworth's poem The White Doe of Rylstone.

After witnessing the immense power of Linton Falls, cross over the footbridge and swing right through a stile (G.R. 003 634). The route now follows the Dales Way

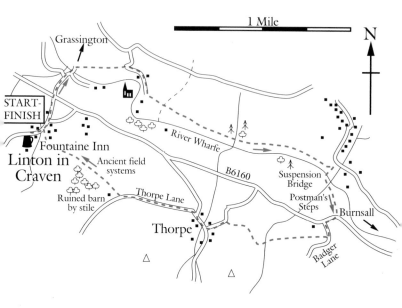

footpath never far from the river. The pre-Norman
church of St. Michael and All Angels rests quietly beside
the river on the opposite bank. At the third stile proceed
right along the metalled road for a short way to rejoin
the wonderful riverside meadows all the way to Hebden
suspension bridge (G.R. 025 624).

Cross the bridge (it sways considerably!) turn left then,
immediately after crossing a footbridge, turn right and
ascend the Postman's Steps - a fit postman, eh?

Continue straight on from the top of the steps, soon
reaching a road - turn right. This road is often very busy,
do take care. Walk facing the oncoming traffic for a short
distance then enter a narrow lane (the first) on the left.

This is Badger Lane, although there's no sign to confirm this. A short way into the lane two adjacent stiles are reached and our route climbs up through the right hand one. Easy now!

From the stile a well defined path leads through several grazing pastures, linked by gated stiles, eventually emerging onto a road (G.R. 015 618), here swing left to enter the hidden village of Thorpe, or to give it its Sunday name, Thorpe in the Hollow. Notice the round-topped hills surrounding the village. These are mounds of limestone, known as reef knolls or drumlins, formed aeons ago when the dales area was a warm lagoon.

The final two miles (3.3km) of this ramble commences by veering right and following the road out of Thorpe in a northerly direction. After a short, upward section swing left at the road junction then follow the metalled lane (Thorpe Lane) to a stone step stile on the right beside a ruined barn (signposted Linton) (G.R. 005 622). This is almost three-quarters of a mile (1.2km) along the lane.

From the stile, head across the pasture towards some trees, where wonderful views are presented of Grassington and several of the higher Wharfedale fells appear. Also notice the terracing in the fields around you. These are strip lynchets, Anglo-Saxon agricultural field systems.

Several stiles are encountered in the final mile (1.6km) en-route to Linton, navigational problems shouldn't ensue. The working dairy farm is unavoidable I'm afraid.

RED LION

This ramble offers delightful riverside segments at the beginning and end. Between these are high moorlands above Hebden and Hebden Gill. An exciting expedition indeed!

DISTANCE:
6 miles (9.6km)
ALLOW:
3 hours
MAPS: Stile
Maps
Grassington
Area, O.S.
Outdoor
Leisure 10
TERRAIN:
Riverside.
Moorland
section on
outward leg
PARKING:
Large car-park
in village

The Red Lion (01756 720204) has long been recognised as a high-standard establishment. Bar meals and sandwiches are available all year, between 12-2.30pm and 6-9pm. Real ales are served and there are log fires and beamed ceilings. The hotel is alongside the River Wharfe close to the superb five-arch bridge, facing south towards Burnsall Fell. It's thought that the hotel originated as a ferryman's inn about 300 years ago. You are requested not to wear walking boots, and dogs are not admitted.

Most popular walk books contain a visit to Wharfedale's former principal lead-mining area - Hebden Gill. This route offers a variation on that popular theme, presenting the 'connoisseur' with an outing rich in contrasting scenery.

Begin from the Red Lion close to the splendid five-arch bridge. The riverside footpath starts from the west end of the bridge, and almost at once you'll pass the rear of St. Wilfrid's church on the left.

Along this tranquil stretch of the river Wharfe were sites of three ancient holy wells. These wells were used in times when baptisms took place in the river instead of inside the church. The wells were dedicated to St. Wilfrid, St. Margaret and St. Helen. There's no visible evidence. Thruskell Well, in lower Hebden Gill is another such example.

Follow the clear path alongside the river all the way to Hebden suspension bridge, passing Loup Scar and Postman's Steps en-route. Cross the suspension bridge, erected in 1887, then take the stile to the left and swing

right, leaving the river
to a gate 200m across
the field. The gate leads
to a road which is
followed for a short
distance to the right, before
turning left into Hebden
Mill Gill (G.R. 026 624).
Pass between the
renovated houses,
following the gravel
path to emerge alongside
some fish tanks on your
left, soon after passing
through a small gate. At
this point it's time to leave
Mill Gill and veer right up
a steep, grass bank to
arrive at a wall corner
(G.R. 028 626). A
signpost (Bank Top)
confirms the direction
towards a large barn.
Pass to the right of the
barn then, still climbing,
seek a gate at the top left
corner of the enclosure. Two
high ladder-stiles in quick
succession, then a gate, lead
to Bank Top Farm (G.R. 035
631).

Another ladder-stile, to the left of

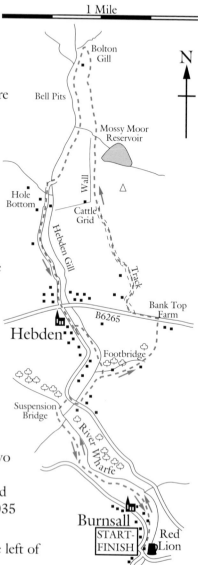

the farmhouse, leads on to the main Grassington-Pateley Bridge road; turn left. Take care as you follow this busy road towards, but not into, Hebden village. Turn right into a rough vehicle track signposted Loss Gill. This track rises steeply and soon offers rewarding views.

Looking SW two noticeable natural features stand out: the conical shaped hills which surround the tiny village of Thorpe are drumlins or reef knolls, formed by mounds of extremely pure limestone and deposited aeons ago.

When the gradient levels out and a cattle grid is reached (don't cross the cattle grid), veer right, leaving the main track to pick up the moorland path running alongside the gritstone wall to your left (G.R. 028 638). This path soon passes Mossy Moor Reservoir, built during the lead-mining boom of the 19th century. Continue in the same line, passing through a succession of gates before gradually descending to arrive alongside Hebden Gill at the confluence with Bolton Gill (G.R. 027 654).

The return to Hebden village is straightforward. Simply follow the beck downstream to Hole Bottom - a small group of houses (G.R. 024 641). The best path is on the left side of the beck. From Hole Bottom follow the road to Hebden village, keeping straight on after crossing directly at the junction. Walk past the tiny post office, then the former village school and turn left at the iron Victorian kissing-gate just beyond on your left. This path leads downhill into the higher reaches of Hebden Mill Gill and soon joins the footpath which was used earlier.

For the return to Burnsall simply retrace your footsteps down Hebden Mill Gill, re-cross the suspension bridge and finally stroll along the riverside.

WHITE HART

Easy walking with plenty of interest, including a long delightful stretch beside the river and a pleasing woodland section.

DISTANCE:
5 miles (8km)
ALLOW:
3 hours
MAP: Stile
Maps, Chevin
Area
TERRAIN:
Easy
PARKING:
Close to Pool
Bridge, or pub
by arrangement

Pool in Wharfedale lies two miles (3.3km) north of the Roman road running between Adel and Ilkley. The village has Anglo-Saxon origins, meaning pond or marsh. The White Hart building was originally a farmhouse, owned by John Milnthorpe (1725-78), taking its name from the White Hart Hotel, which stood opposite the farmhouse. The licence was transferred to the farmhouse in 1825, then under the ownership of Miss Susannah Scott. The White Hart is reputed to be haunted! Food is available all year during the following hours: Monday-Thursday 11am-9.30pm; Friday-Saturday 11am-10pm; Sunday - 12-9.30pm. Tel 0113 2843011.

Leaving the White Hart car-park turn right, walking through the village and over the road bridge (G.R. 244 456). Notice the parish boundary inscriptions near the centre of the bridge - Leathley and Pool.

On the right, at the end of the

bridge, a signpost indicates the way alongside the river. This delightful section is followed for a mile (1.6km) to join Castley Lane - turn right.

Arthington viaduct, on the Leeds to Harrogate line, is prominent across the river. The viaduct was built around 1880, being part of the Leeds-Thirsk railway. Stride along Castley Lane seeking the access road into Ings Farm (G.R. 263 463) on the left.

Head on the access road, but as the farm buildings are approached ignore the temptation to veer right; instead go straight on, seeking a waymarked gate on your right which isn't obvious. Don't use the gate directly ahead which bears a no entry message.

Beyond the gate swing left, accompanying the fence through several fields and an enclosure containing redundant farm implements to

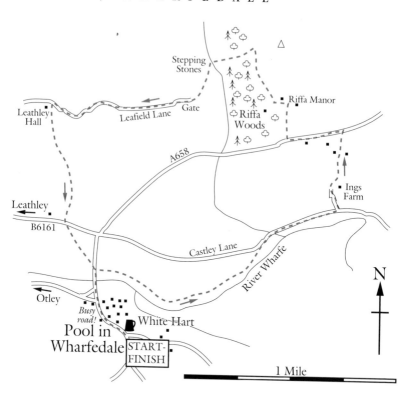

emerge at farm drive via a waymarked gate. Turn right and follow the drive to the main A658 road - cross over, turning left. The next half mile (800m) is alongside the busy road, so do take care.

Swing right at a signpost into the drive of Riffa Manor (G.R. 258 467). Riffa Woods are to your left as the drive continues, eventually veering left beyond the entrance to Riffa Manor. After passing a second residence leave the drive and pass through a waymarked gate on your right. This leads into Riffa Woods.

Follow a well-trodden path which briefly leaves the woods, turning left alongside the fence. After 250m re-enter the woods through a gate, then head downhill noticing the remains of an old packhorse route and the Indian Chief stone approximately halfway down the incline on the right. The three-foot stone, resting on the ground, has an outline and indentations which give it the appearance of an American Indian Chief.

On reaching the bottom cross the new (1994) footbridge, leaving the wood at a stile, before crossing Riffa Beck directly ahead, by the large stepping stones (G.R. 253 472).

Then follow an obvious track, rising to an upright stone post. From the post swing left for a few metres before making diagonally right across the field to a gated lane known as Leafield Lane.

This ancient route is followed for a mile to Leathley Hall (GR. 237 468). [A permanently damp section en route is unavoidable]. Immediately prior to arrival at the hall, swing left to pass to the rear of the property, noticing the duck pond within the grounds. At the end of the enclosed section hop over a stile then, walking with the boundary on your left, locate another stile. Cross this, veering right, and proceed across several fields to the B6161 road.

At the road go left, then after several hundred metres over a stile on the right. This leads diagonally left across the field with Pool Bridge in sight. From the bridge walk through the village to the White Hart, taking extreme care when crossing the road.

SUN INN

The stiff half-hour climb out of the unique and interesting village of Dent is rewarded with some excellent views of Dentdale and the surrounding countryside.

DISTANCE:
5 miles (8km)
ALLOW:
3 hours
MAP: O.S.
Outdoor Leisure
Map 2
TERRAIN:
Well-defined
tracks
PARKING:
Large car-park
in Dent

The Sun Inn is typically Dales with charming public rooms, original beams and comfortable furnishings. A Dent Brewery House, selling traditional ales, the Sun provides a variety of bar meals. It is open Monday-Friday 11am-3pm (food until 2pm) and 7-11pm (food until 8.30pm); Saturday-Sunday open all day (food noon-2pm).

The singular village of Dent resting in the south-eastern most corner of Cumbria (formerly North Yorkshire) contains many noteworthy features and a wealth of historical interest. Indications of this tidy, remote village's character are instantly evident as you leave the car-park and stride onto the cobbled, narrow streets. The prevailing mood is of times long past and quaintness.

The narrow streets thread their way through the village with its shops, tea-rooms, post office and public houses. There's an abundance of neat, white cottages too. An air of friendliness and local pride abounds. Dent has a rather fine parish church - St. Andrew's - the tower being rebuilt in 1787 from materials used in the original Norman construction. A century later the whole church was restored at a cost of £3,000 with money raised by public subscription.

Inside the church there are many interesting features, including the Sedgwick memorial window in the eastern wall, the old box pews and the chancel floor - laid with Dent marble, creating a chess board effect.

Adam Sedgwick is Dent's most famous son. He was born in

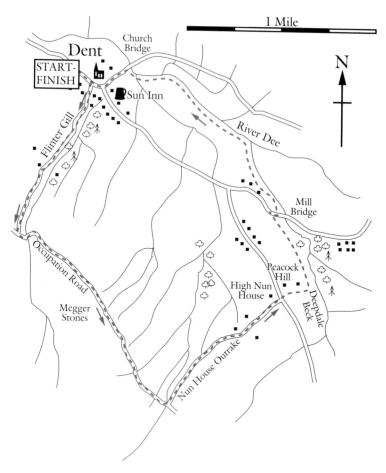

1785 at the parsonage and became Professor of Geology at
Cambridge University, a position he held for 55 years.
Sedgwick died in 1873 and is interred in the chapel of
Trinity College. There is a large memorial to him,
fashioned from Shap granite, outside the church gate.

The long-time redundant marble industry flourished in Victorian times, but floundered when cheaper Italian marble was imported. Another long-forgotten industry synonymous with Dent, was knitting. During the 18th century everyone was involved in this occupation, knitting stockings for the military. It's recorded that the noise made by the clicking of needles was deafening. Other tales tell of needles being put down to cool! The populace became known as "the terrible knitters of Dent", no reflection on the quality of their work.

Start this interesting and invigorating ramble from the main car-park in the centre of Dent. Cross the road and enter the lane to the left of the village school. Follow this lane unerringly, past the village green into Flinter Gill. A signpost on the green confirms the way.

The metalled surface stretches to the last cottage - Ghyll Head - then abruptly ends. From here the way becomes narrow, uneven and steep! Flinter Gill, a spectacular, wooded ravine, conceals a dramatic, tumbling watercourse. The path demands a stiff, uphill climb all the way from Dent, but offers sensational retrospective views. These views adequately compensate the physical efforts called for during the ascent.

The uphill section lasts about 30 minutes, ending at a junction with a broad, enclosed track known as Occupation Road. A name acquired around 1860, when many upland fells were being enclosed or "occupied".

Close to this junction (G.R. 698 858) there's a memorial

seat, donated by the friends of John H. McNeil, who died aged 39.

Swing left along the "ocky", south-easterly for about one and a half miles (2.4km) to reach a pronounced bend. At this point leave the "ocky", turning left through a gate-signpost Nun House Outrake (G.R. 711 846).

The ensuing mile (1.6km) is downhill, following a steep, uneven trackway that's often wet and slippery. Please take extra care on this descent.

Towards the bottom, High Nun House farm is on the left, then when a road is reached cross straight over into the confines of Peacock Hill Farm (G.R. 719 855). The way through the pastures is waymarked but careful attention is required. The path runs adjacent to, but not alongside Deepdale Beck, making towards Mill Bridge (G.R. 721 861).

Arriving at the road bridge go left across the road and simply follow the riverside footpath back to Dent. This final section is the well-trodden route known as the Dales Way. (A long distance footpath between Ilkley and Windermere.)

The riverside path leads into the outskirts of Dent at Church Bridge (G.R. 707 872). Turn left and follow the road through the village to the car-park.

GAME COCK

Follow the old packhorse route from picturesque Austwick to the fascinating village of Clapham. Views along this route are outstanding.

DISTANCE:
4 miles (6.4km)
ALLOW:
2½ hours
MAP: O.S.
Outdoor
Leisure Map 2
TERRAIN:
Easy
PARKING:
Roadside

The walk begins from the Game Cock public house in the pretty Dales village of Austwick (G.R. 766 686). The pub is popular with walkers as the village is ideally situated for several interesting treks in all directions. The pub serves lunch between 11.30am-2.30pm and evening meals from 7-8.30pm. Availability of meals differs during the winter months. However, at the time of writing the pub was about to change hands and I therefore advise walkers to ring the Game Cock on 01524 251226 before making plans. There is little room for parking at the pub and you are asked to take care where you leave cars on the roadside in the village.

Emerging from the Game Cock turn left, following the road out of the village. Take the second-left turning after the school, soon passing through the confines of Town Head farm (G.R. 770 688). Beyond the farm climb steadily before passing through a well-tended garden, where lawn protectors have been laid to minimise damage. A stile leads into a

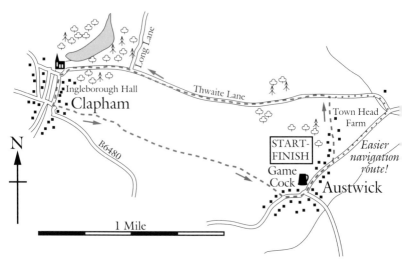

large field; follow the wall to your right, noticing the wonderful views.

Locate a ladder-stile in the far right hand corner of the field (G.R. 771 693). This leads into a wide, uneven track known as Thwaite Lane, formerly a packhorse route linking Clapham and Austwick with Horton in Ribblesdale. Entering Thwaite Lane turn left and follow its course all the way into Clapham.

The village of Clapham is a wonderful place to visit, but it's often extremely busy. Thousands of tourists arrive here, particularly in summer, seeking the many attractions. These include the beck and its bridges, Ingleborough Cave, the Farrer Nature Trail and much more.

A U S T W I C K ,   C R U M M A C K D A L E

You enter the village in the most unusual manner - descending through two large tunnels! These were built by the brothers James and Oliver Farrer in 1833, being part of extensive alterations to the family estate. The Farrers formerly lived in nearby Ingleborough Hall, which is currently an outdoor activity centre.

After sampling Clapham's charm and delights, embark on the return leg to Austwick, following the signpost outside the public toilets near the entrance of the large car-park.

The route to Austwick is straight forward and requires

little explanation. A succession of stiles lead across the meadows on a well-defined footpath and nothing more needs to be said.

However, distances displayed on the signposts are somewhat confusing. The first post indicates Austwick $1\frac{1}{4}$ miles. The next post announces Austwick $1\frac{1}{2}$ miles. The exact distance is further confounded at Austwick. The signpost there illustrates Clapham 2 miles! Emerging from the fields at Austwick turn left for the final half a mile (880m) to the Game Cock and refreshments.

VICTORIA

An impressive walk in Malhamdale and Airedale including the tourist honeypot of Malham village. There are extensive views of this beautiful limestone area.

DISTANCE:
7 miles
(11.3km)
ALLOW:
3-4 hours
TERRAIN:
Easy. Field paths
and roads
MAPS: Stile
Publications -
Malhamdale,
O.S. Outdoor
Leisure Map 10
PARKING:
Room for
several cars on
roadside to
Hanlith

Set in the quiet and picturesque village of Kirkby Malham, the Victoria provides a welcoming refuge from the tourist magnet of Malham. With an extensive range of real ales available, the pub also offers sandwiches and bar meals between noon-2pm and 7-9pm. Between November 1 and Easter, the pub opens in the evenings only. Parking for walkers by arrangement only on 01729 830213.

With your back to the Victoria turn right and walk along the lane, passing the church and vicarage which, the plaque reveals, was restored in 1866. At the end of the lane with a cottage named 'Clock' facing, turn left along the road. This rises quite steeply and the more "athletic" can claim this to be the first hill of the day!

Ignore the entrance on the right leading to New Close Farm, continuing uphill for about a quarter of a mile (400m). When the road eventually levels out, seek a gate on the right which leads to Acraplatts Farm (G.R. 886 615). There's a signpost too - Malham 1½ miles. This is the route to follow.

While here notice the old, stone mile-post on the left of the road. The inscription is badly eroded but with care you can make it out. One side reads "To Settle" the other "To Kirkby Malham".

After passing through a second gateway and a small plantation on the left, there is a ladder-stile on the right just before another plantation.

Cross the stile then head off down the field, towards a

ruined barn. A stone step-stile right of the gate gives access to the field holding the ruin. Pass to the left of the ruin, towards a telegraph pole. Just beyond the pole there's a stile. Hop over this and follow the direction of the drunkenly tilted signpost. With Acraplatts Farm on your left, head across the field diagonally left, towards a ladder-stile (and tilted signpost). From this stile walk directly ahead towards the brow of the hill, where another ladder-stile comes into view.

Leave this stile, walking downhill, with the wall on your right to yet another ladder-stile alongside a barn (G.R. 888 624). Follow the wall on your right to another ladder-stile.

From here head in a straight line downhill, passing an abandoned farm on the right, to a signpost standing isolated in the field. Malham Cove and Malham village are in your sights.

Leaving the signpost walk with the wall on your right towards a stile with a large barn close by. The remaining route into Malham needs no explanation but problems could arise if there's been heavy rainfall. A lively stream may have to be navigated. Fortunately two "clapper" bridges are available to ensure dry feet!

Having inspected the delights of Malham, leave the village, crossing the "clapper" bridge alongside the blacksmith's (opposite Sparth House Hotel) (G.R. 901 628).

Having crossed Malham Beck - not the infant river Aire - swing right to follow the Pennine Way to Hanlith. Quite soon the path leaves the waterside and rises - don't be

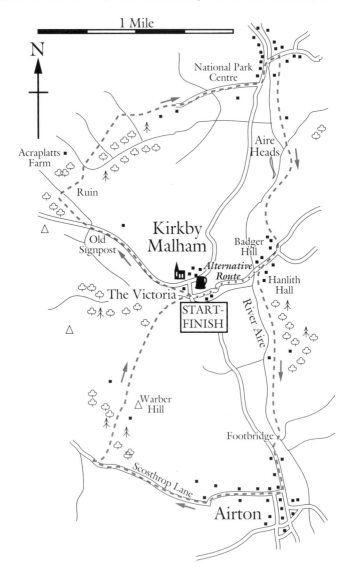

1 Mile

N

National Park Centre

Acraplatts Farm

Ruin

Old Signpost

Kirkby Malham

Aire Heads

Badger Hill

Alternative Route

The Victoria

Hanlith Hall

START-FINISH

River Aire

Warber Hill

Footbridge

Scosthrop Lane

Airton

deterred, follow it to a ladder-stile alongside a tree. (The river Aire begins its journey at a point known as Aire Head, G.R. 902 623.)

The way continues across a depression in the landscape, heading to the next stile near a group of trees. Crossing this, your passage will be counted, this being a pedestrian counting stile (clever stuff). A signpost sited at the wall corner indicates the way, then after 50m notice the short yellow waymarker in the centre of the field. A second marker verifies the way, making towards the buildings. A waymarked gate, left of the buildings, quickly followed by a gated stile gives access onto the road. Veer right - downhill to Hanlith. Arrival in Hanlith reveals Hanlith Hall (1892) and Badger Hill, an impressive dwelling which displays a bronze figure of St. Francis of Assisi in the gable wall.

At the bridge (G.R. 900 612) a choice of routes is presented. Those who are weary and in need of urgent sustenance can simply follow the road over the bridge and reach Kirkby Malham within half a mile (880m). For the more adventurous and those prepared to undertake a further 3½ miles (5.6km), hop through the stile and follow the Pennine Way alongside the river Aire. Note: It is imperative that you keep close to the riverside. Eventually you'll encounter a waymarked gate, leading you out of one enclosure and into another. You must pass through this gate.

Having completed that crucial manoeuvre, head across the field, now ignoring the Pennine Way route, towards a substantial footbridge upfield and to the right. Airton, the next objective, is in sight. Cross the footbridge then follow the grass track to a gate. Turn left into Airton following the road. Having entered the confines of Airton, take the first major turning right. There's a small triangular green and a signpost displays Settle 6½.

This is Scosthrop Lane and is followed (passing Scosthrop House, then Moor End Farm) for almost a mile (1.6km) until adjacent signposts are met. One points to Otterburn 1½, the other to Kirkby Malham 1 mile - the latter the obvious choice.

Follow the line of the wall initially, until a signpost close to some trees urges you left, heading uphill to the left of a cluster of trees. Beyond the trees is a stone step-stile (G.R. 888 601). This is Warber Hill, a prominent viewpoint.

Head off downhill, accompanying the wall. Ignore the signpost to Airton, but soon after is a small, gated-stile. This leads you downhill to a tiny flat bridge. Cross this then go diagonally left across the field - a signpost on your right will confirm your line. Make towards the right of a plantation and a stile to the penultimate enclosure. Kirkby Malham is within reach now but do take care - the next stile is concealed in the wall at the bottom end of the field. Cross the last field to a tiny gate which leads you back to the Victoria.

MASON'S ARMS

The walk takes in Embsay Crags (371m) and a stiff, energy sapping climb to the summit is involved but your physical efforts will be well rewarded. with fine, long distance views from the top.

DISTANCE:
4¼ miles
(7.2km)
ALLOW: 2½
hours
MAPS:
Outdoor Leisure
Map 10.
Southern area.
TERRAIN:
Meadows and
Moorland. Steep
climb to
Embsay Crag
PARKING:
Mason's Arms,
by arrangement

Nestling beneath Embsay Crag, the Mason's Arms is a 400-year-old hostelry steeped in character. Situated in the reclusive hamlet of Eastby, between Barden Towers and Embsay, the Mason's Arms offers traditional Yorkshire ales and food all year between 12-2pm and 7-9.30pm. Tel 01756 792754.

The games room overlooks the old village jailhouse and an etching on a window relates to the poignant story of trooper Mason a local man who fought in the Boer War. Athol Mason engraved his name and number on the window before setting off to war. He survived but the trauma of war left him disturbed and eventually he took his own life by throwing himself in nearby Spindle Mill Dam.

Pub landlord at the time, John Lister, dived in to recover Mason's body but when he found that Mason's jacket pocket was full of stones he pretended not to find the body, as suicide was considered shameful. Mason's father found out about the deception and offered £10 to any man who broke the window containing his son's inscription - the window is intact today.

From the Mason's Arms car-park turn left and follow the road for a short distance, to a horse trough on the right-hand side. Directly opposite you'll find a red letter-box set into the wall to your left, at this point swing left. There are two signposts both pointing in the same direction - Draughton and Low Lane.

Proceed down the lane with a high wall to your right, then after negotiating a right hand bend, there is a farmyard. Walk straight ahead into the farmyard, swing left and pass through a waymarked gate (G.R. 017 543). Go through the gate, cross a small grassed area which leads onto a well defined farm road and turn right.

As you walk along the farm road St. Mary's, Embsay, comes into view across the fields and quite soon Rowton Beck accompanies you on the right.

Soon the roadway swings right, crossing over the beck, towards a gate alongside a large oak. At this point leave the roadway, heading straight on across a pasture, making for the gap between the large bungalow and the boundary wall. Pass through a narrow stile, alongside the large gate (G.R. 014 537), leading onto the road - turn right. The walk now leads through the more modern part of Embsay, although several older premises remain, identified by their lintel datestones. The more recent developments have been tastefully constructed. A good example is the houses built in the street named Low Bank to your left, shortly before reaching the junction of Main Street and Kirk Lane. Continue straight ahead along Main Street, passing a succession of delightfully named cottages - Jasmine Cottage, Dove Cottage, Wistaria Cottage, Penyghent Cottage - soon followed by the Methodist church and Scissors Cottage displaying a datestone of 1693. Across the road the war memorial and the village hall are observed just before veering right, into the car-park (G.R. 009 538).

Pass through the tiny car-park to a gate, then head

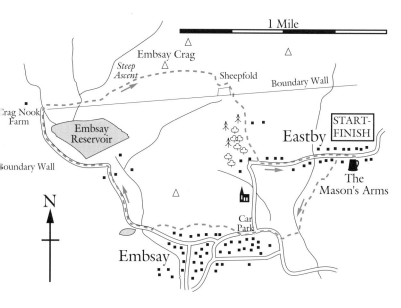

diagonally left across a field towards a signpost and a stile in the far corner. Embsay Crag, the pinnacle of the walk, is very prominent at this point. Don't be deterred!

The way forward is well signposted across several fields linked by stiles, and navigational problems shouldn't ensue. After passing a silage store, often covered with numerous car tyres, pass through another stile then head diagonally right towards the angle of a rickety looking fence. Just beyond this point and left of a telegraph pole is a concealed stile. From here make towards a gate/stile, then head straight on through the final field to a stile, left of a gate.

The stile gives access onto a road - turn right. Notice the mill pond over the wall to your left, as you begin to follow the road unerringly towards Embsay reservoir, about half a mile (800m) away. Embsay Crag looks a daunting prospect! As you walk along this section you'll pass the entrance to Intake Farm and some time after you'll see the chimney at the former Spindle Mill. The embankment of the reservoir is soon encountered and a signpost points the way left to Embsay Crag 1 mile (G.R. 001 545). Follow the uneven track beyond the water to reach a stile and a signpost indicating Embsay Kirk and Crag (G.R. 995 548). Hop over the stile and head along the obvious bridleway. After a short way a signpost invites you to veer right and to follow the blue waymarkers to Embsay Crag (G.R. 005 552).

The route is well waymarked but problems may arise because the waymarkers are three feet tall - the bracken can be almost double that height! The golden rule is to keep making upwards and you can't really avoid the crag. After catching your breath and enjoying the panoramic views, head off eastwards, descending on a clear track while making for the wall which divides the moorland from the pastures. On the way down look back and admire the imposing outline of Embsay Crag.

Arriving at the wall, which is just 10 minutes walk from the crag, follow on in the same direction, soon reaching a stone sheepfold. Just beyond this is a gate where the signpost indicates a footpath and bridleway to Eastby (G.R. 009 553).

Head off downhill, accompanying the wall to your right to a gate on the left of a tree plantation. From here the way back requires little instruction. Keep walking downhill, passing Bondcroft Farm, to arrive at the main road. Turn left and follow the narrow, busy road back to the Mason's Arms - about a 10-minute walk. Take care on this final section.

On the final descent, unavoidable evidence of environmental desecration is clear to see, in the form of a huge limestone operation.